# SIKH SHRINES
## IN
## PAKISTAN

By
KHAN MOHAMMAD WALIULLAH KHAN

KALPAZ PUBLICATIONS
NEW DELHI-110052

**SIKH SHRINES IN PAKISTAN**
*(Religion, History, Archeology)*

ISBN: 81-7835-013-0



Published in 2000 in India by
Kalpaz Publications
C-30, Satyawati Nagar
Ashok Vihar Phase-III
Delhi-110052
E-Mail: kalpaz@hotmail.com

Laser Typeset at A.S. Printers
Printed at Mehra Offset Printers, New Delhi

# CONTENTS

## ILLUSTRATIONS

# PREFACE

Soon after the independence, the Department of Archaeology undertook a survey of all the important monuments protected under the Ancient Monuments Preservation Act belonging to pre-historic, Buddhist, Hindu and Muslim periods of our history. A survey of such other monuments which inspite of their historical importance and architectural merits were not protected was also carried out. During the course of this survey, it was observed that barring a few, Sikh monuments, being of recent origin, were not listed for protection in the past.

Moreover, Sikh Gurdwaras forming integral part of Sikh religious and social life and for the traditions of sanctity associated with them, were managed and looked after by well knit Sikh organizations. After independence the management of Sikh Shrines was disrupted and therefore, the responsibility for their maintenance and repairs fell on the Government of Pakistan. This all the more necessitated a preliminary survey of all the Sikh Shrines in Pakistan by the Department of Archaeology.

I am thankful to Mr. Mohammad Wali Ullah Khan, Superintendent of Western Pakistan Circle, Lahore for the great pains he has taken in the collection and compilation of the information about the Sikh Shrines included in this memoir which may serve as a basis for any work desired to be carried out on the subject.

F. A. KHAN
Director of Archaeology
Pakistan

# SIKH SHRINES IN WEST PAKISTAN

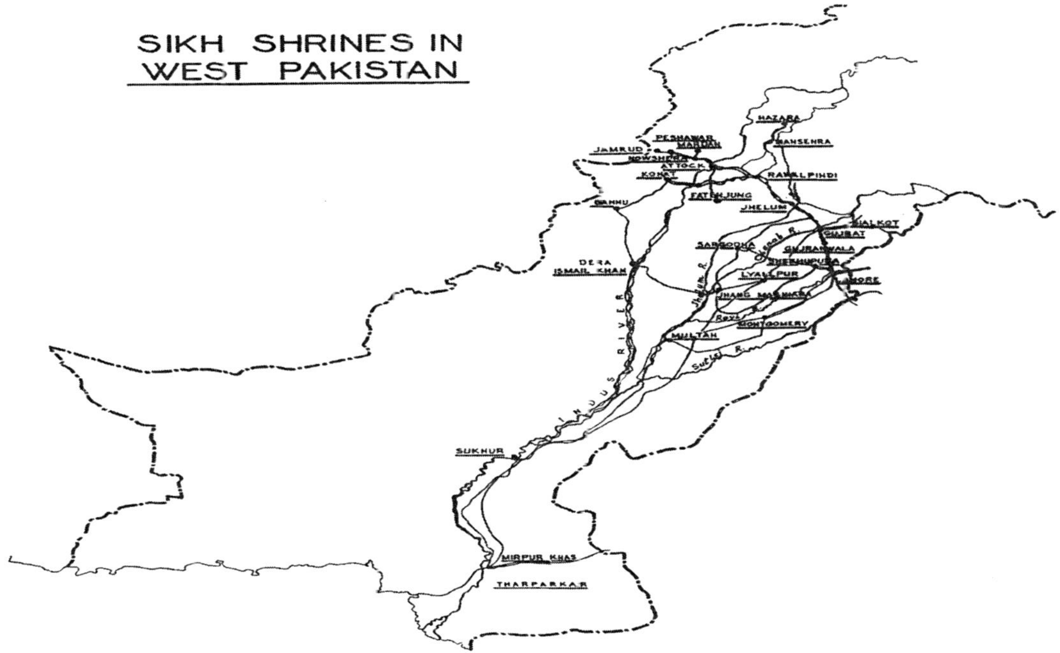

# INTRODUCTION

In this memoir an attempt has been made to describe briefly the important Sikh Shrines in West Pakistan. These Shrines fall into two distinct categories: (1) those specifically associated with the Sikh Gurus and (2) those held sacred for other reasons. Each category of the Shrines has been arranged districtwise in alphabetical order. Brief life sketches of the Gurus are given before the description of Shrines associated with them. A consolidated list of all the Shrines has also been given at the end.

The Sikh Gurdwaras are more than a place of worship. They serve as schools, a meeting place and a rest-house for travellers in addition to enshrining the Granth Sahib. The Gurdwaras are, as such, integral part of the Sikh religious and social life. After independence, the responsibility and care for proper maintenance and repair of Sikh Shrines fell on the Ministry of Rehabilitation and the Department of Archaeology. This necessitated the undertaking of a special survey of all the Sikh Shrines in West Pakistan.

The present work is not intended to present a study of the architectural genius of the followers of Sikhism which has its roots in the areas comprising West Pakistan. Nankana Sahib, where the great Sikh apostle Guru Nanak was born in 1464, is situated in the centre of West Pakistan. Sikhism like Buddhism, Jainism and all other religions which arose in the Indo-Pakistan sub-continent was the product of the reaction against the dominant Brahamanism and its rigid caste system. But another important factor which influenced the mind of people who contributed to the growth of Sikhism, was the impact of Islam which had spread to Iraq, Turkistan, Persia and Afghanistan and came into contact with Christianity, Judaism, Buddhism, Zoroastrianism and above all neo-Platonic philosophy. This impact resulted in the emergence of the school of theological intellectuals who lived in monasteries spending their time in religious and philosophic discourses. To this school belonged the group of Sufis who advocated the inclusion of non-muslims in their group. The success of Sufism in winning over non-muslims in the sub-continent was phenomenal. Their toleration, not only quickened the pace of breaking of the shackles of Hindu caste system but also influenced the Hindu philosophy and was responsible for the evolution of the Bhakti movement, propounded by Chaitanaya in the east, Tukaram, Namdev and Trilochan in Central India, Ramanand, Mirabai, Tulsidas and above all Kabir in the north. The Sikh religion is in fact a product of the Sufi and Bhakti schools of thought. Guru Nanak was greatly influenced by Kabir and Shaikh Ibrahim Farid (1450—1535) a descendant of the famous Sufi saint Shaikh Fariduddin Shakarganj of Pak Pattan whose works were incorporated in the Granth Sahib. Guru Nanak studied books of Hindu and Muslim religions and it was only after deep study of both the religions that he evolved his own school of thought. Accompanied with two followers, a Hindu peasant and a Muslim musician, Guru Nanak went round preaching, composing sermons in verse, which his Muslim companion set on music. His preachings were intensely monotheistic and largely directed against the pretensions of priest-hood. His success in forging Hindus and Muslims together was so immense that on his death his body became a subject of dispute—the Muslims wanted to bury it after the Muslim rites while the Hindus wished to cremate it. He was regarded as a Sufi or Darvesh by Hindus and Muslims alike.

In the early stages of the growth of Sikhism the Gurus were greatly favoured by the Muslim rulers. Guru Nanak and Angad, enjoyed universal respect. Guru Ram Das who had good relations with Emperor Akbar, prayed for his victory of the formidable stronghold of Chittor Garh. Akbar visited the Guru and bestowed upon him the land on which was built the Golden Temple of Amritsar. The Gurus had so far refrained from taking part in politics and were solely devoted to religious activities. But with the accession of Guru Arjun Dev, started the second phase of Sikhism when its followers took to costly attires and organised themselves into a military unit. Guru Arjun Dev, however, maintained amicable relations with Muslim saints like Mian Mir Sahib of Lahore, who is said to have laid the foundation stone of the Golden Temple of Amritsar. Personal enmity arose between the Guru, his brother Pirthi Chand and the Hindu Finance Minister of the Mughal Governor of Lahore. The situation became complicated when unfortunately the Guru sided with Khusru, son of Emperor Jahangir, who had rebelled against his father. This was a political issue which created some sort of misunderstanding between the Guru and the Mughals. The next Guru, Har Gobind was the first to take up arms against the Mughals and in most of his encounters, his forces were generally conducted by Muslim Officers. The name of Painda Khan, one of his ablest lieutenants, is well known. The Guru solemnised his marraige, built a grand house and a mosque for Painda Khan at Govindpur. Jahangir for purely political reasons got him arrested but it was Mian Mir Sahib again, who reconciled the Guru and Emperor Jahangir.

His successor Guru Har Rai made an alliance with Dara Shikoh, the eldest son of Shah Jahan. This displeased the Moghul Emperor Aurangzeb but the matter was hushed up with an explanation which was given by the son of the Guru. Har Krishan became the next Guru in 1661 at the age of six and died of small pox in 1664. He was succeeded by Guru Tegh Bahadur, who mustered a well equipped force and tried to establish an independent principality for which purpose he formed a league with Shaikh Adam Hafiz, a disciple and successor of Shaikh Farid II. Both of them were opposed, defeated and arrested by the imperial forces. The Guru was taken to Delhi and detained. During the course of his confinement the Guru volunteered to perform a miracle whereby the executioner's sword would fail to sever his head from body. As the legend goes, the Guru wrote some words on a piece of paper and tied it round his neck like a charm. But it so happened to the horror and surprise of all those assembled on the occasion, that when sword struck the neck, the head was severed and on examining the message on the charm it was found to read *'Sar diya par sirr na diya'*— 'gave the head but not the secret'. Guru's death in these circumstances was not due to any religious bias, but on account of a political issue. Aurangzeb who for political reasons could imprison his father, ill-treat his own brothers and sons, could not of course be expected to have spared any rival who would have challenged his authority. The tenth and the last Guru, Gobind Singh, was the founder of the militant Sikh theocracy. In his exploits against the Hindu Rajas of the northern hills principalities, the Guru's army comprised of a large number of pathans. He had friendly relations with the Pir of Sadhaura and other Muslim spiritual heads. On Aurangzeb's death the Guru threw his lot with Bahadur Shah whom he helped to defeat prince Azam. After his death the Khalsa were enjoined to look upon the Granth Sahib as the living Guru, as no new Guru was to come after him. The subsequent history of Sikhs presents an interesting picture of a rising political power at a time when the Mughal rule started declining. It will thus be seen that the struggle between the Mughals and the Sikh Gurus was not struggle between two religious factions, but it was a tussle for political power between the two.

The basic principles of Sikhism are much closer to Islam than to Hinduism. But as it happened in the case of all the religious orders of the sub-continent, except Islam, Sikhism also absorbed elements of Hinduism.

A study of the life, events of the Gurus and the large number of monuments sacred to them will, however, reveal how deeply all the Sikh

Gurus in general and Guru Nanak, Arjun Dev and Har Gobind in particular are associated with Pakistan.

It is therefore, in the larger interest of Pakistan's history and culture, that as a first step towards preserving the sacred relics of the Sikhs, the present Monograph has been prepared.

I am thankful to the district authorities of West Pakistan for assisting me in collecting the information about Sikh Shrines and I am also indebted to Mr. Ishtiaq Khan, Custodian, Archaeological Museum, Mohenjodaro for his assistance in the compilation of the Monograph. Thanks are also due to Mr. Abdul Aziz Qureshi, Photographer, Department of Archaeology.

I deem it a great privilege to thank Dr. F. A. Khan, Director of Archaeology, Pakistan for permitting me to undertake the job and providing me with all the facilities for compiling this publication.

*Lahore* MOHAMMAD WALIULLAH KHAN

*Guru Nanak Sahib*

**PLATE NO. 1.**

*CHAPTER I*

# SACRED SHRINES ASSOCIATED WITH THE GURUS

## GURU NANAK SAHIB

## (1469—1539)

NANAK, son of Mehta Kalu Chand, a Khatri of Bedi sub-caste (gotar) and Tripta Devi, was born in 1469 A.D., during the reign of Sultan Bahlol Khan Lodhi. He is generally believed to have been born at village Taluandi, presently known as Nankana Sahib, in District Sheikhupura, but another account states that he was born at the house of his mother's parents at Kana Kacha, 15 miles from Lahore and Lahore-Firozpur Road and was as such called Nanak, (i.e., a boy born at Nanke, residence of mother's parents). Nanak's first teacher, it is said, was Maulvi Qutubuddin. It is also stated that he was carefully educated by Sayyid Hasan, a wealthy but childless neighbour. Others believe that Mehta Kalu, a Patwari by profession, sent him to Pandit Gopal to learn Persian, the language in which all accounts and state documents were maintained. Pandit Baij Nath is mentioned to have been his Sanskrit teacher. It is said that Nanak's father tried his best to impart worldly education to his son who from the very childhood possessed saintly habits, mystical ideas and a reflecting mind. However, there are sufficient reasons to believe that he acquired sufficient knowledge of the Holy Quran as well as Hindu Shastras.

In 1488 A.D., at the age of sixteen, he was married to Bibi Saulakhni, daughter of Lala Mool Chand Khatri of Pakhoke in District Gurdaspur, according to others of Batala. He had two sons; Sri Chand born in July, 1494 A.D. and Lakhi Chand born in February, 1497. Sri Chand founded the sect of Sikh ascetics known as Udasis and Lakhi Chand preferred to live in pleasure. Kalu Chand tried to introduce Nanak to business but in vain. Nanak's mother therefore sent him to his brother-in-law Diwan Jai Ram (husband of Nanki) who was the Manager (Karinda) of Sultanpur State (Kapurthala Area) under Daulat Khan

Lodhi. There, he is said to have served as a Manager of Modi Khana, for about 17 years (?). There after he abandoned his home and travelled extensively for about 15 years (?) to attain real wisdom by meditation, by study and by enlarged intercourse with mankind. He is said to have travelled over the whole of India, and visited Ceylon, Afghanistan, Persia, Turkistan, Mecca, Medina and Baghdad. Traditions assert that while at Baghdad he was presented with a robe with Quranic verses interwoven in its fabric. The robe, called *Chola Sahib*, is still preserved at Nankana Sahib as a sacred relic. During these travels he had several companions, among whom, Mardana, the rababi or harper, Lahana, who later succeeded the Guru, Bala, a Hindu Jat and Ram Das alias Buddha, are the most frequently referred to. At last this wandering minstrel returned to his native land, discarded ascetic life and passed his remaining life as a family man and as a religious teacher. His preaching was intensely monotheistic and largely directed against the pretension of priest craft. He believed in universal toleration through which he sought to bring Hindu and Muslim together. Nanak combined the best ideas of preceding reformers. He believed in transmigration of soul and its final dwelling in bliss. He places salvation in good works and uprightness. He earnestly felt that religion was for the service of mankind and not the mankind for the service of religion. However, he did not interfere with Hindu rituals which continued to remain in vogue among his followers. As for himself, he adopted the way of Sufism, a fact reflected in almost all of his paintings wherein he is generally depicted in the dress of a Muslim saint, holding a rosary in his hand. He had close associations with a number of Muslim Saints. He developed intimate friendship with Shaikh Farid, a renowned saint, and one hundred forty-two stanzas composed by him (Shaikh Farid) were later incorporated into the *Adi Granth* (First book) itself.

In the later days of his life he settled down at Kartarpur, which he founded on the west bank of River Ravi near Jessar in Narowal Tahsil of Sialkot District and died there at the age of 70 on the 10th of Asuj, 1596 Vikrama Era (1539 A.D.) leaving behind an army of zealous and admiring disciples.

## ATTOCK DISTRICT

### 1. GURDWARA PANJA SAHIB AT HASAN ABDAL.

The story of 'Panja Sahib' is told variously, but the gist is as follows:—

Once Baba Guru Nanak, happened to visit Hasan Abdal. Here on the top of a hill lived Baba Wali Qandhari a Muslim Saint (according to others Yar Ali). Baba Wali Qandhari, also known as Baba Hasan Abdal, a descendant of the Sayyids of Sabzwar, visited Punjab with Mirza Shah Rukh son of Taimur, sometimes between 1408 to 1447 A.D. Even today, there is a small whitewashed shrine (*baithak*) attributed to this Muslim Saint. Guru Nanak coming to the place asked one of his disciples to fetch water from the spring. The water was, however, refused by the saint. Thereupon Baba Guru Nanak miraculously made the spring to abandon that place and to flow from the spot where he was standing. The Muslim Saint was much annoyed with the intruder and rolled down a rock to crush him. Guru Nanak, however, gently stopped the missile by the push of his open hand. The hand left an impression on the rock (Pl. No. 2). Subsequently this rock became an object of great reverence for the followers of the Guru who started calling it Panja Sahib.

During the reign of Ranjit Singh the trans-Indus territory was annexed by Hari Singh Nalwa who constructed a temple with a tank on this spot. Later on the temple was replaced by a two storied building with beautiful frescoes in the interior depicting life stories of Guru Nanak and other gurus. In 1928 the Gurdwara Parbandhak Committee took over the management of the Shrine and built a new and magnificent three storied temple (Pl. No. 3) in grey sandstone in place of the old shrine. The tank was also enlarged and rebuilt in marble. Around the temple there is an open space paved with marble. On the four sides of this open quadrangle are brick built double storey buildings, which provide accommodation to the pilgrims and the establishment. In the middle of the southern side there is a two storied spacious hall.

The new temple building is designed after the style of the samadh of Maharaja Ranjit Singh at Lahore, a mixture of Hindu and Muslim architectural features culminating in a distinctive character, which may, for its individual effect, be named as Sikh style.

The site of Panja Sahib is a sacred spot from the Buddhist times. During the early part of 7th century A.D. when Hiuen Tsang, the Chinese Traveller visited this place; here stood a tank of limpid water sacred to Naga King, Elapatra and also a Buddhist monastery, the remains of which still exist, and as in the case of all ancient places imbued with sanctity, this site continued to be sacred although the creeds went on changing.

Since after independence, the Department of Archaeology have considerably improved the surroundings of the holy shrine by converting the area lying between the Panja Sahib and the so-called Lala Rukh's Tomb into a blossoming garden.

## GUJRANWALA DISTRICT

### 2. CHAKI SAHIB (Pl. No. 4)

During his campaign against the Lodhi Dynasty of India, Babar assaulted and destroyed Saidpur, now known as Eminabad, in the Gujranwala District. There was a general massacre of Pathan as well as Hindu inhabitants. Guru Nanak's life was spared but he was taken a prisoner and was condemned to grind corn for which purpose a hand mill was supplied to him. The mill, however, miraculously revolved byitself and Guru Nanak had only to put the corn in it. The miracle was reported to the Emperor who after a discourse with the Guru set him as well as all captives of Saidpur free. Babar is said to have remarked that he would not have destroyed the city had he known that such holy men were to be found there.

The mill is venerated by the Sikhs and is placed in a gurdwara known as Chaki Sahib.

### 3. GURDWARA RORI SAHIB AT EMINABAD (Pl. No. 5)

Guru Nanak, during his stay at Eminabad, is said to have made his bed on a platform of rori (pebbles or broken stones). This platform became a place of veneration and later on when Sikhs came to power a gurdwara was built over it. This gurdwara, an imposing building of cut brick work, is a place of great sanctity. Some of the roris (stones) preserved in the gurdwara are still shown to the faithfuls on the occasion of Baisakhi and Diwali fairs held in April and October every year.

### 4. KHOI BHAI LALU AT EMINABAD

Guru Nanak, while at Eminabad, stayed with a carpenter named Lalu and used the water of a well situated in his house. The well or Khoi is held sacred and is known as Khoi Bhai Lalu.

## GUJRAT DISTRICT

### 5. GURDWARA KIR BAWA SAHIB AT JAI SUKH, TAHSIL PHALIA (Pl. No. 6).

This place was visited by Baba Guru Nanak and is therefore held sacred. The gurdwara was originally built by Bawa Bhag, an Udasi saint.

## JHELUM DISTRICT

### 6. GURDWARA CHOA SAHIB AT ROHTAS

A spring used to flow close to the fortification wall of Rohtas Fort. Guru Nanak is said to have ordered the spring to emerge and flow for the public use. A gurdwara was built close to the spring during the Sikh period. The gurdwara was extended and renovated recently.

## LAHORE DISTRICT

### 7. DERA AT CHAHAL, POLICE STATION BARKI

Dera Chahal is known to have been the residence of the parents of Guru Nanak's mother. Moreover Nanki his elder sister, is also said to have died at this place. The Guru visited this place very often. This gurdwara was built to commemorate the association of the Guru with the town.

### 8. DHARAMSALA CHHOTA NANKIANA AT ALPA, TAHSIL LAHORE; (Pl. No. 7)

This Dharamsala situated at village Alpa, Tahsil Lahore is called Chhota (smaller) Nankiana, and is associated with Guru Nanak.

### 9. DHARAMSALA CHHOTA NANKIANA AT MANGA; (Pl. No. 8)

This Dharamsala was built in memory of Guru Nanak, who by his preaching, enlightened a Hindu ascetic at this place. Guru Har Gobind is also said to have visited this place on his way to Amritsar after visiting Nankana Sahib.

## 10. DHARAMSALA SAT GURU NANAK, LAHORE; (Pl. No. 9)

While describing Chaki Sahib at Eminabad in district Gujranwala, it has been mentioned that Baba Nanak was detained and later set free by Babar when he captured Saidpur. This event seems to have taken place in 1526 A.D. and soon after his release at Saidpur, Baba Nanak came to Lahore.

When Babar captured Lahore, Guru Nanak had already reached the town and was staying at this place, which is situated in Mohalla Kakezaiyan near Chaurhatta Mufti Baqir. During the sikh rule a dharamsala was built here. Inside the building there is a L shaped hall with a platform. On the farther end of this hall is a marble-paved gallery. The carved-wood beam of this gallery bears a Gurmukhi inscription in bold relief. A marble slab in the centre, surrounded by the sacred emblem of the Sikhs is also inscribed with a Gurmukhi inscription. The dharamsala is built in brick and lime mortar.

## 11. GURDWARA AND TANK AT VILLAGE JAHMAN, POLICE STATION BARKI; (Pl. No. 10)

Guru Nanak while on his way to Chahal and back, used to halt at the pond of this village. The pond is now converted into a tank and the gurdwara built near the village is known as Rori Sahib. A famous devotee of Baba Sahib named Surya and some Bhabras i.e., Jainis who had accepted Sikhism, lived here.

## 12. GURDWARA AT GHAWINDI, POLICE STATION BARKI; (Pl. No. 11).

Once Guru Nanak came from village Jahman to Ghawindi. During his stay there a child was born to a Banjara. Congratulations were offered to the parents who entertained the neighbours. The son died after a few days. The Banjara and his relatives were then seen weeping and wailing. The Guru seeing the parents of the child overwhelmed first with joy and then with grief composed a verse in Sri Rag under the title '*Phre Chand Shabd*' depicting the vicissitudes of life. Later on, a gurdwara was built in memory of Guru's stay.

### 13. GURDWARA AT KANGANPUR, TAHSIL CHUNIYAN

Guru Nanak during the course of his first journey came to Kanganpur where the villagers did not allow him to halt and also played practical jokes on him. This treatment did not annoy Guru Nanak who instead prayed for the welfare of the village saying, '*was de raho*' (May you remain here). On being subsequently questioned, why he blessed the village in which he was not allowed to stay, he replied that if the people of this village were disturbed and moved to other place, they would ruin it by their inhuamn conduct, so it was in the interest of others that they might stay where they were. The tree under which he reposed for a while is known as Mal Sahib.

## MONTGOMERY DISTRICT

### 14. GURDWARA AT DIPALPUR; (Pl. No. 12)

Enroute to Multan, Baba Nanak stayed at Dipalpur under a withered pipal tree which, however, turned green, produced leaves and blossoms to provide shade to Baba Sahib. At this very place a leper named Nuri was also cured. The pipal tree is still green and Nuri's grave can also be seen nearby.

The gurdwara built here during later Sikh Period is known as 'Nanikiyana'. An annual fair used to be held here.

### 15. GURDWARA NANAK JAGIR, TAHSIL OKARA; (Pl. No. 13)

This place is said to have been visited by Guru Nanak. The present gurdwara was later built to commemorate the event. Repairs to gurdwara had been carried out by the Rehabilitation Department, Government of Pakistan.

### 16. GURDWARA NANAKSAR AT HARAPPA; (Pl. No. 14)

Guru Nanak during one of his journeys went to Harappa. The ruler of this place was a tyrant and injustice prevailed in the country. Guru Nanak advised him to be merciful and kind to his subjects. During this visit the Guru stayed under a Jand tree and distributed water among those present there. A gurdwara and a tank were constructed here to commemorate the event.

### 17. GURDWARA TIBBA BABA NANAK SAHIB AT CHAK I/EB, TAHSIL OKARA; (Pl. No. 15)

Guru Nanak is said to have visited and stayed at this place. A fair used to be held here annually.

## MULTAN DISTRICT

### 18. GURDWARA DIWAN CHAWALI MASHAYKH AT CHAK 317, TAHSIL VEHARI; (Pl. No. 16)

Baba Guru Nanak, during his stay at Multan, visited this place where then lived the Diwan of Chawali Mashaykh. He is said to have meditated and stayed with the famous Muslim Saint Hazrat Baba Farid Ganj Shakar at this place. Later this gurdwara was built. A fair also used to be held here annually.

## SHEIKHUPURA DISTRICT.

### 19. GURDWARA BAL LILA AT NANKANA (Pl. No. 17)

It is said that Guru Nanak during his childhood used to recite '*Sat Kartar*' while playing with children of his own age. On the spot, where he first played and subsequently spent nights in meditations, Rai Buller, the landlord of the village built a small tank in the affectionate rememberance of the childhood of the Guru at a time when his fame had spread far and wide. The tank was enlarged by Kaura Mal, Diwan of Zakaria Khan, viceroy of Lahore, in the middle of 18th century A.D. The present imposing Gurdwara was, however, added at a later date.

### 20. GURDWARA JANAM ASTHAN AT NANKANA; (Pl. No. 18)

Guru Nanak is generally believed to have been born here. A large gurdwara was built in his memory during the Sikh Period which has been modified and enlarged several times. This gurdwara, is held in great veneration by the Sikh community. In this gurdwara ,one of the many invaluable sikh relics kept is the sacred cloak (Chugha) known as *Chola Sahib.* The cloak embroidered with Quranic verses is said to have been presented to the Guru by the ruler of Baghdad when he visited him. The gurdwara was thoroughly repaired by the Government of Pakistan in October, 1959.

### 21. GURDWARA KIARA SAHIB AT NANKANA; (Pl. No. 19).

Once Mehta Kalu sent Guru Nanak to herd the buffaloes in nearby forest. All worked well for the first day. On the second day he fell asleep and the unattended cattle trespassed on the adjoining field and damaged its standing crop. The owners remonstrated Guru Nanak and lodged a complaint to Rai Buller, who summoned Guru Nanak and his father and inquired about the matter. Guru Nanak said that no damage had been done to the crop and that it has rather been blessed by God. Rai Buller is said to have either sent his men to the spot or himself visited the field and to his astonishment found that not a single blade was trampled or eaten by the herd and field was green and fresh.

The field where the miracle took place is venerated by the Sikhs and a gurdwara stands there encircling the area once under cultivation.

## 22. GURDWARA MAL JI SAHIB; (Pl. No. 20).

While herding the cattle Guru Nanak used to take rest under the shade of a tree. Once Rai Buller happened to pass that way and observed that the protecting shadow of the tree had remained stationary over the Guru and did not change like the shadows of other trees with the sun's progress. On another occasion he found a cobra protecting the saint with its hood.

The tree which is known as Mal Ji Sahib is held sacred by the Sikhs. A gurdwara was built after its name with a view to enclose the sacred tree. The tree under which the Guru stayed in Kanganpur, Tahsil Chuniyan, is also called Mal Ji Sahib.

## 23. GURDWARA MAULVI PATTI, NANKANA SAHIB; (Pl. No. 21)

It is said that Mehta Kalu sent Guru Nanak to a Maulvi to learn Persian in the feign hope that if he knew the court language he might be able to earn his livelihood. He astonished his teacher by copying the alphabet from memory after one day, and while answering the questions of Maulvi Sahib, he himself assumed the role of a teacher and composed an acrostic on the letters of the Persian alphabet. The present gurdwara marks the place of his discourse with the Maulvi Sahib.

## 24. GURDWARA SACHCHA SAUDA (REAL BARGAIN) AT CHAUHARKANA; (Pl. No. 22).

Once Mehta Kalu, father of Guru Nanak, gave fifty rupees to Nanak and asked him to purchase profitable merchandise. While passing near Chauharkana forest, he noticed a party of mystics who were starving for three days. Guru Nanak purchased edibles for the whole amount and distributed the food among the starving mystics.

On his arrival at home, his servant Bhai Bala who had accompanied him, related the story to Mehta Kalu who was much annoyed and asked for Nanak's explanation. Guru Nanak told him that he was asked to purchase profitable merchandise and that he had purchased the best merchandise for the life to come. This incidence is known as '*Sachcha Sauda*' or the Real Bargain. Later on Maharaja Ranjit Singh, in order to commemorate this event of Nanak's life, built a gurdwara at the present site.

## 25. GURDWARA TAMBO SAHIB NANKANA; (Pl. No. 23)

On his return from Chauharkana (Ref. S. No. 24 above) Guru Nanak was censured by his servant for his recklessness with his father's money. He realised how wrongly the nature of his act would be understood and instead of going home direct sat under a tree out side the village of Taluandi. He was found by his father at this place and was cuffed for disobedience. The old tree under which he sat is still preserved and is known as Tambo Sahib, a corruption from Thamb meaning trunk and support. Later a gurdwara was built in the commemoration of this event.

(Note) All the Gurdwaras at Nankana Sahib are maintained by the Rehabilitation Department, Government of Pakistan.

# SIALKOT DISTRICT.

## 26. GURDWARA BAIRI SAHIB AT SIALKOT; (Pl. No. 24)

Baba Nanak, during his visit to Sialkot gave spiritual guidance to Hamza Ghaus, a Muslim saint. Here, Baba Nanak is said to have stayed under a Bairi (plum) tree. This present gurdwara built at the site of the Bairi tree is situated at a distance of about two miles of the eastern outskirts of the town on Sialkot-Pasrur Road. It was rebuilt by Raja Ranjit Singh who also endowed a large estate for its maintenance. This gurdwara, which has a beautiful guilded dome, also contains the Samadh of Natha Singh Shahid.

The gurdwara is in an excellent state of preservation and a caretaker has been appointed to look after it by the Government of Pakistan.

## 27. GURDWARA BAOLI SAHIB, AT SIALKOT.

This gurdwara lies in the western skirts of Sialkot City at a distance of about one furlong from the Sialkot-Daska Road. The Baoli Sahib (a large well with a flight of steps descending down to the water level) was built in memory of Guru Nanak who visited this place on his return from Afghanistan.

## 28. GURDWARA DARBAR SAHIB AT KARTARPUR; (Pl. No. 25).

This gurdwara is situated on the western bank of River Ravi near Jassar in the Narowal Tahsil. Baba Nanak after return from his wanderings in quest of truth, settled down at Kartarpur where he died in 1939 A.D. In the year 1911-12 Lala Shyam Das built the present gurdwara and residential quarters.

(N.B.) Annual repairs to the monument are carried out by the Rehabilitation Department and the Government of Pakistan have also appointed a caretaker to look after this important Sikh Shrine.

## GURU ANGAD—THE 2ND GURU

### (1504—1552 A.D.)

Guru Angad, earlier known as Lahana, was the son of Lala Phero Mal, a khatri of Tirlahan Got r and Sobhar Devi. He was born at Mati Ki Sarai, now known as Nanka Ki Sarai in Ferozpur District in Samvat 1561 (1504 A.D.). In the year 1531 A.D., while going to pay a visit to Devi's Temple at Kangra, he heard of Guru Nanak and went to pay his respects to him. He was deeply impressed by the Guru and became his devotee. He served the Guru with utmost devotion. When Guru Nanak foresaw his end approaching near, he is stated to have made a trial of the obedience and merits of his chosen disciples and after careful consideration preferred the simple and sincere Lahana and appointed him as his spiritual successor in preference to his own sons and named him Angad, an abbreviation of the Persian word *Ang-e-Khud* i.e. part of his own body. Angad succeeded Guru Nanak in 1539 A.D. on the latter's death. Guru Angad did creditable work for the propagation of Sikhism. Writing of Janam Sakhi, the life account of Baba Guru Nanak, introduction and development of Gurmukhi characters and committing to writing the sayings and deeds of Guru Nanak which he heard from the Guru Nanak's old companion, Bala Sindhu, are the most meritorious work of Guru Angad to the service of the Sikh faith. Later on his writings were incorporated into Adi Granth, 'the first book' which was finalised by Guru Arjun Dev, the 5th Guru.

Guru Angad was married to Bibi Chimi of Khadur village in Amritsar District where he finally settled. He had two sons, Dasu Ji and Dattu Ji, and one daughter. Dattu was issueless while the descendants of Dasu Ji are called Bawa Khatris. Guru Angad died at the age of 48 years in Samvat 1609 (1552 A.D.) at Khadur where stands his Samadh attached to a gurdwara. He appointed Amar Das, an assiduous follower as his spiritual successor in preference to his own sons.

No sacred place associat.d with this Guru is situated in Pakistan.

*Guru Angad*

PLATE NO. 26.

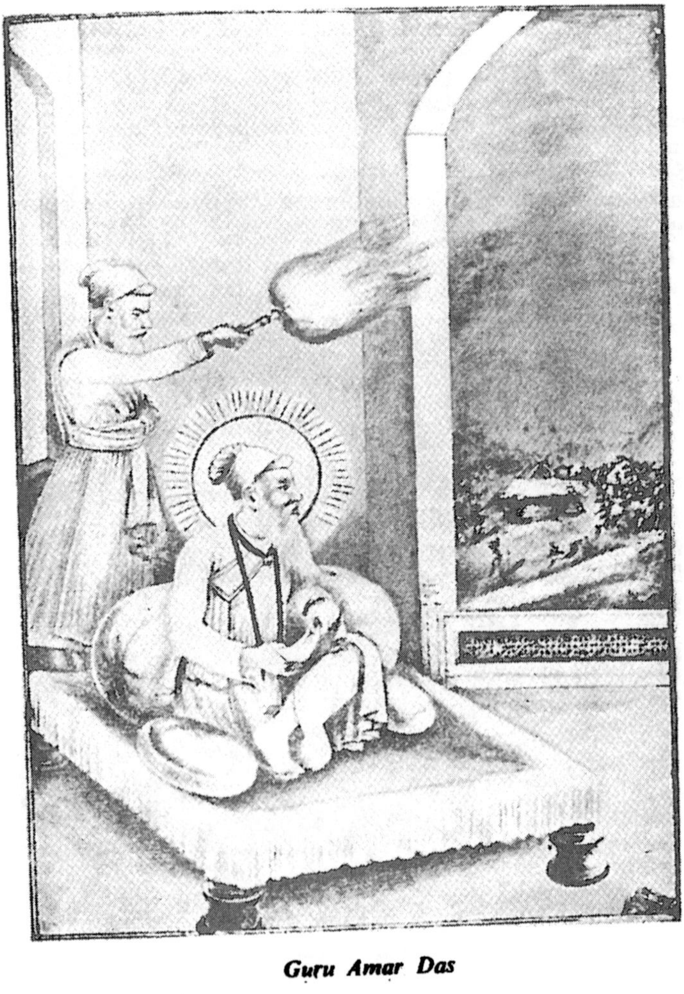

*Guru Amar Das*

**PLATE NO. 27.**

# GURU AMAR DAS—THE 3RD GURU

## (1509—1574 A.D.)

Amar Das, son of Tej Bhan, a Khatri of Bhalla Gotar was born in Samvat 1566 (1509 A.D.) at Basar in Amritsar District. According to some authorities the date of his birth is Samvat 1536. In Samvat 1597 (1540 A.D.) he was so much impressed on hearing a Bani (speech-verse) composed by Guru Nanak, being recited by Bibi Amro, daughter of Guru Angad that he met Guru Angad and accepted Sikhism. He served Guru Angad so devotedly that the Guru appointed him as his successor whom he succeeded in 1552 A.D. Guru Amar Das spent much of his life in Govindwal, a village close to Khadur in Amritsar District, and died there in 1574 A.D. at an age of sixtyfive years, after serving the faith for twenty-two years.

Sri Chand, son of Guru Nanak, after being deprived of the spiritual succession to his father, renounced the world and adopted the life of a mystic and became the founder of the Sect of Udasis, a community indifferent to the concerns of worldly life. His influence grew day by day and many a Sikh were drawn towards him. Guru Amar Das realizing the danger of his ever growing popularity preached with great enthusiasm the middle path between asceticism and worldly life, setting his own example and quoting the precedents of the two former gurus, who had neither renounced the world nor indulged too much in its pleasures. He at last succeeded in exterminating the influence of Udasi cult from the Sikhs and saved the new community from lapsing into the fold of a limited group of monks. In order to organise the propagation of new faith he divided the country into twenty-two *Manjas* (divisions) and appointed one pious Sikh at the head of each *Manja*. This was rather the first organised efforts towards establishment of the Sikhs as a community. He also strongly dissuaded his fellows from performing the Hindu ritual of *Sati*.

Amar Das had two sons and one daughter. It is said that for his great love for his daughter and for the services of her husband, Ram Das appointed his son-in-law as his successor in preference to his own sons.

No sacred place associat d with this Guru is situated in Pakistan.

## GURU RAM DAS—THE 4TH GURU

## (1534—1581 A.D.)

Ram Das was born in Samvat 1591 (1534 A.D.) at Chuna Mandi, Lahore. He married Bibi Bhani, daughter of Guru Amar Das the 3rd Guru, in A.D. 1555 and settled at Govindwal with his father-in-law. Guru Amar Das was much impressed with his untiring zeal and devotion to the faith and as a token of great love for his daughter, selected him to be his successor in preference to his own sons. On the death of Guru Amar Das in 1574 A.D., he succeeded him as the 4th Guru. It is said that he prayed for Akbar's victory over the formidable fort of Chittor, and Akbar, as a token of respect, paid a visit to him. Akbar is also said to have bestowed a piece of land upon the Guru where the latter started construction of the sacred tank known as 'Amritsar', the pool of immortality. Besides the sacred tank, he also started the construction of the temple, but did not survive to see it completed. The temple and surrounding locality was, later, named Ramdaspur after him.

He died in 1581 A.D. after serving the Sikh faith for seven years and was succeeded by his son Arjun Dev.

Janam Asthan described below is the only place in Pakistan sacred to the memory of this Guru.

### JANAM ASTHAN GURU RAM DAS, LAHORE; (Pl. No. 29)

It is situated on the east of Dera Baba Khuda Singh in Chuna Mandi. A street separates the two buildings. The whole complex of the building covers an area ot 122'.6"x97'.6". On the west is a spacious courtyard paved with black and white tiles. A flag staff stands in the north western corner near the flight of steps.

On the ground floor are shops which form part of the Chuna Mandi Bazar. It is a double storied building, square in plan, covering an area of 41'.3". The approach is through a small door on the west. It is a well balanced building; its lower part contains sunken panels enfaced with marble upto a height of 12 feet. In the middle of the facade of upper

*Guru Ram Das*

PLATE NO. 28.

storey facing west, there is a slightly projecting balcony with three openings, flanked by balconies similar in style on either side. The interior of the hall is paved with hexagonal marble tiles in black and white. In the centre stands a marble platform. On all sides of the hall there is a gallery at a height of 12 feet from the floor. The ceiling is of carved wood work embellished with mirrors. Along the sides and in the corners there are eight rooms, four of them on sides, each measuring 12′×10′; the other four approached by the corners, each measuring 7′x7′. All these rooms are paved with white and black marble tiles.

## GURU ARJUN DEV—THE 5TH GURU

## (1563—1606 A.D.)

Arjun Dev, the youngest son of Guru Ram Das, was born in 1563 A.D. and succeeded his father in 1581 A.D. His elder brother Pirthi Chand, disputed the succession and made representations against his supersession to the Mughal Emperor Akbar, who refused to intervene. Emperor Akbar and Prince Salim held Guru Arjun in high esteem and the latter conferred upon the Guru a considerable area of revenue-free land at Kartarpur.

Guru Arjun Dev started reforms in Sikh polity and religion, and selected Amritsar as the centre of the Sikh community. Here he completed the digging of the sacred pool (Amritsar) and finalised the construction of the sacred temple Darbar Sahib started by his father. Uptill now the Sikhs used to offer *nazarana* (offering) in cash and kind to the gurus. Guru Arjun Dev regulated these offerings into a systematic tax which was collected through men specially appointed for the purpose to twenty two *manjas*. The amount collected was paid to the Guru in a great darbar held annually on the occasion of Baisakhi at Amritsar. Guru Arjun Dev compiled and arranged the writings of his predecessors under the title *Adi Granth* (the first book). With the gradual increase in his power and authority he is alleged to have started interfering with the affairs of the state. In 1605 A.D. when Prince Khusru revolted against his father, Emperor Jahangir the Guru is said to have helped the rebellious prince not only with his blessings but also with money. Khusru was, however, defeated and captured. Pirthi Chand, the elder brother of Arjun Dev, who had earlier unsuccessfully contested the Guruship and Chandu Lal, the Diwan of Lahore, to whose daughter the Guru had refused to betroth his son, exploited the situation and exaggerated the part played by the Guru in inciting Khusru's revolt. The Emperor ordered that the Guru's case be decided in accordance with the *Yasa* the law of Changez Khan. The Guru was fined rupees two lakhs which he was unable to pay and as such was given in the custody of Diwan Chandu Lal. The Guru had to undergo great rigours and hardships at the hands of Diwan Chandu Lal and at last died in June 1606 A.D. According to the most popularly accepted account of his death by the Sikhs the Guru obtained permission

*Guru Arjun Dev*

PLATE NO. 30.

to take bath in the river Ravi and disappeared miraculously when he dived in the stream.

That the Guru died from the tortures inflicted by Chandu Lal is first referred by Mohsin Fani, author of *Dabistan-e-Mazahib*, a contemporary scholar and friend of Guru Arjun Dev's son Guru Har Gobind. This is one of the earliest and most authentic reference throwing light on Guru's martyrdom and clears the misunderstanding that Emperor Jahangir was responsible for Guru's death, by clearly mentioning that Chandu Lal who seizing the opportunity of non-payment of fine by the Guru and further instigated by Pirthi Chand, the unscrupulous brother, tortured Guru to death. It may be said that as head of the state Jahangir was responsible for the action of his officers but the fact, that the Sikhs records testify, that on hearing about the inhuman treatment meted out to Guru Arjun Dev, Chandu Lal was handed over to Guru Har Gobind, the son and successor of the Guru, to be treated by him as he liked. It shows that Jahangir was extremely sorry and annoyed at this tragic event and as an act of exemplary punishment, he handed over the offender to the aggrieved.

## LAHORE DISTRICT

### 1. BUDDHU KA AWA (KILN), LAHORE; (Pl. No. 31)

The old kiln belonged to a brick manufacturer named Buddhu. The bricks of this kiln could not be fully baked due to a curse inflincted on it by a Sikh Saint Bhai Lakhu. The poor owner prayed to Guru Arjun Dev who gave him a blessing. It is said that it was due to this blessing that the ill-baked bricks were sold at a higher price. The kiln has long since disappeared but its site, near Gulabi Bagh Gateway, on Shalamar Road has been preserved as a protected monument and is being maintained by the Archaeological Department.

### 2. DIWAN KHANA (SITTING HALL), LAHORE

Guru Arjun Dev is said to have built a Diwan Khana for religious assemblies in Chuna Mandi. The old structure was replaced by Maharaja Ranjit Singh by a new building which now bears No. H/2145 in the records of Corporation of Lahore. The Diwan Khana is spread over an area measuring 102′x89′. In the northern portion, facing the bazar, there are a few shops. In the south-east corner there is an old well now blocked and used as a *Sabi*. In the centre is a brick paved courtyard measuring 62′x 30′. The floor of this hall is paved with marble tiles in black and white and the rest in red concrete. The western part of the hall contains a marble platform bearing an inscription in Gurmukhi.

### 3. GURDWARA BAOLI SAHIB, LAHORE; (Pl. No. 32)

A Baoli with steps descending to the water level existed to the west of the Golden Mosque of Bhikari Khan. The baoli was built by Guru Arjun Dev with the money presented to him by Chhajju Bhagat. A '*langar khana*' (place where free food is supplied) was also attached to it . It is said that during the time of Guru Har Gobind, the Baoli no longer in use, was filled up, the langar khana closed and a mosque built, at the site. In 1834 A.D. Maharaja Ranjit Singh fell ill and his astrologers advised him to excavate the Baoli and take bath from its water. The mosque was therefore pulled down and the Baoli re-opened. A tank was also added. The site of the Baoli is marked with the construction of a memorial gateway.

### 4. LAL KHOI, LAHORE; (Pl. No. 33)

It is said that Guru Arjun Dev during the period of his internment in the house of Chandu Lal, Diwan of Lahore, used to take bath from the water of this well whose diameter is about 10 feet. The well is situated in Mochi Gate. The only evidence of its antique character is the use of small country bricks in its lower part. It is now enclosed by cement Jalis and the parapet is finished with cement plaster.

### 5. SAMADH, LAHORE; (Pl. No. 34)

The Shrine of Guru Arjun Dev is situated opposite the Lahore Fort, north-east of the Samadh of Maharaja Ranjit Singh.

As mentioned above Guru Arjun Dev, according to Sikh belief, disappeared miraculously in the waters of Ravi. To commemorate the event, Guru Gobind (1606-1645 A.D.) arranged the construction of a small shrine here and appointed Bhai Langaha to look after it. Later Maharaja Ranjit Singh reconstructed the shrine by the present Samadh with its heavily gilded dome.

The entrance to this shrine is through a door set in marble in the east. An ornamental flying marble arch in front of the door marks the beginning of a court (53'x41') paved with white and black marble tiles. Immediately to the right is a gold painted flag-staff fixed on a marble base.

To the left a flight of marble steps leads into the verandah of the Samadh. The verandah, which surrounds the main square sanctuary (15'-6") is finished with marble facing with three cuspid arched openings supported on slender double marble columns. The ceiling of the verandah is decorated with floral and pictorial paintings in tempra. The main roof has a heavy and crowded niched balustrade which is topped with gumbadis. On the four corners there are square burjis with domes. The pride of the monument is the Naga pusht heavily gilded bulbous dome with a towering pinnacle. On the four corners of the dome were added small burjis '*guldastas*' to balance the main dome. All the pinnacles of domes of the main sanctuary bear sun flowers which are also gilded.

To the west of the courtyard is a hall with a marble platform measuring 9'-10"x4'-10"x1'-2"; the seat for Granth Sahib and the Granthi. It has a gallery running round three sides at a height of 10'. The gallery is approached by marble steps leading from the passage to the west of the sanctuary. A sun shade of red sand stone supported on brackets of the same material run along the roof of the hall. A fair is annually held here on the anniversary of Guru Arjun when a large number of Sikh pilgrims visit the shrine. The open space in front of the Samadh has been converted into beautiful grassy lawns by the Lahore Corporation.

### 6. GURDWARA AT HANJRA, TAHSIL CHUNIYAN; (Pl. No. 35)

Two Sikh brothers named Jatri and Hanjra founded two villages after their names. There arose a quarrel between them regarding the boundaries of their villages. Consequently Guru Arjun Dev went to the spot and settled the dispute. This gurdwara was built to commemorate the visit of the Guru Arjun Dev.

### 7. GURDWARA AT JAMBAR KALAN; (Pl. No. 36)

Guru Arjun Dev is said to have visited this place and converted to Sikhism, Kidara Samdu, Mukanda, Tulsa, Lalu and others during his stay. About one hundred and fifty acres of land is attached to this gurdwara.

## SHEIKHUPURA DISTRICT

### 8. GURDWARA AT HAFT MADAR (Pl. No. 37)

Bhai Ladara, a favourite disciple of Guru Arjun Dev, resided in this village. He was suffering from some disease. Once he rubbed one of the shoes of Guru Arjun Dev to his body and got cured. This shoe which is still possessed by Bhai Ladara's family is held sacred by Sikhs who believe that it can cure the patients suffering from that disease. A stick of Guru Arjun Dev preserved with the descendants of Bhai Ladara is also held sacred. This gurdwara was built to house the above sacred relics.

*Guru Har Gobind*

PLATE NO. 38.

# GURU HAR GOBIND—THE 6TH GURU

## (1595—1645 A.D.)

Har Gobind, the only son of Guru Arjun Dev, was hardly eleven years of age when his father died in 1606 A.D. His uncle Chandu Shah made vain attempts to ascend the *gaddi*. Guru Har Gobind however was acknowledged as the lawful guru.

The steady growth of power of the Sikh gurus and the incidents such as the alleged help of Arjun Dev to Khusru, in his designs against his father, Emperor Jahangir, led the Mughal court to take cognizance of the situation. Consequently Jahangir thought it administratively necessary to put a check on their growing power. On the other hand Guru Har Gobind, had not only to put up with the Mughal Emperor but to face his uncle Pirthi Chand who was constantly plotting against him. Above all, the bitterness caused by the incident of confinement and death of Guru Arjun Dev was already there.

Confronted with this situation the new Guru thought that the only honourable course left for him was to resort to arms. With a view to infuse martial spirit in his followers the Guru introduced the practice of hunting and flesh eating and laid much emphasis on military training. He also encouraged the offerings of war weapons and horses for his use. He attired himself in martial dress and carried two swords as emblem of leadership, both spiritual and temporal. He also gathered all the paraphernalia of royalty around him i.e. a stable of eight hundred horses, three hundred mounted followers and a bodyguard of sixty men equipped with matchlocks. In Amritsar the Guru built the Akal Bunga (House of God) where he sat on a throne and administered justice like a prince. In short he founded a sort of state within a state.

In the beginning he had cordial relations with Jahangir who placed him in command of seven hundred horses and one thousand men. But on the instigation of Chandu Lal, who represented him as a man of dangerous ambitions, and also for the non-payment of fine imposed on his father, Arjun Dev, Guru Har Gobind was detained and confined in the Gwaliar Fort. He was released on the intercession of the famous Muslim Saint Mian Mir of Lahore.

After Jahangir's death in 1627 A.D. the Guru again became unfriendly towards the Mughals. He reorganised and strengthened his army which consisted of large number of Sikhs, Hindus and Muslims. The author of *Panth Parkash* mentions that Ram Partab, the Raja of Jeysalmer also sided with the Guru. Realising the necessity of safe resort, he built the first Sikh stronghold at Kartarpur (now in Jallundhar District of India). Times and again Mughal forces were sent from Lahore to subdue the Guru but he successfully resisted them at Amritsar, Gobindpur and Kartarpur.

Guru Har Gobind had very cordial relations with some of the Muslim Saints. Mohsin Fani, the author ot *Dabistan-e-Mazahib* who came in contact with him in 1053 A.H. (1634 A.D.), was his intimate friend. Fani says that the account of first five gurus was communicated to him by Guru Har Gobind himself. He had a Muslim Officer named Painda Khan, in his army, on whom he bestowed special favours. He solemnised the marriage of Painda Khan and built a grand house and a mosque for him in Gobindpur. Painda Khan was a valiant soldier and led the Guru's troops in almost all the battles against Mughal armies.

Being mostly engaged in warfare and re-organisation of the Sikhs, Guru Har Gobind could not devote as much time for the propagation ot the Sikh religion as he desired. He died at Kartarpur in 1645 A.D. leaving behind five sons from his three wives. Guru Har Gobind has special liking for his eldest son Gurditta but the latter died during his life time and the Guru therefore appointed his grandson Har Rai as his successor.

## GUJRANWALA DISTRICT

### 1. GURDWARA AT HAFIZABAD; (Pl. No. 39)

Guru Har Gobind, while returning from Kashmir took rest at Hafizabad. A gurdwara was afterwards built here in memory of his stay.

### 2. GURU KA KOTH (ROOM) AT WAZIRABAD; (Pl. No. 40)

During his return journey from Kashmir Guru Har Gobind is said to have stayed with certain Bhai Khem Chand at Wazirabad. The room in which he stayed is known as Guru Ka Koth and is held sacred by the Sikhs.

## GUJRAT DISTRICT

### 3. GURDWARA AT GUJRAT; (Pl. No. 41)

Guru Har Gobind on his way back from Kashmir visited Gujrat and met the renowned Muslim saint Shah Daula. Later a gurdwara was built to commemorate this visit.

## LAHORE DISTRICT

### 4. GURDWARA AT AMAR SIDHO, NEAR RAILWAY STATION KOT LAKHPAT; (Pl. No. 42)

On his way from Mozang to Amritsar Guru Har Gobind visited this place after leaving Mangat. A gurdwara was later built in commemoration of his visit.

### 5. GURDWARA AT BADHANA, POLICE STATION BARKI; (Pl. No. 43)

Guru Har Gobind on his way back from Lahore to Amritsar stayed here and discussed some wordly affairs and religious issues with a Hindu Saint Julhan Bhagat. A gurdwara was later constructed to commemorate this event.

### 6. GURDWARA AT DHISALWAN, POLICE STATION BARKI

Once Guru Har Gobind went to Dhisalwan from village Jhatiyan on preaching mission. A gurdwara was built at the place where he resided while at Dhisalwan.

### 7. GURDWARA AT GURU MANGAT, NEAR RAILWAY STATION LAHORE CANTT; (Pl. No. 44)

Guru Har Gobind halted here on his way back from Mozang to Amritsar. This gurdwara was built in commemoration of his visit.

### 8. GURDWARA AT HADYARAH, POLICE STATION BARKI; (Pl. No. 45)

This gurdwara has been built over a place where Guru Har Gobind halted during his journey to Lahore.

## 9. GURDWARA AT MOZANG, LAHORE; (Pl. No. 46)

Guru Har Gobind resided in Lahore for sometime. His residence at Mozang (now on Temple Road, Bhundpura) was later on converted into a gurdwara. This gurdwara was held in high esteem during the reign of Maharaja Ranjit Singh and is still one of the very sacred places of the Sikhs.

The gurdwara has entrance gates on the northern, southern and eastern sides and is joined by large size buildings on the north-west side. The gurdwara is a double storied hall, measuring 55'x34'--5' raised on a platform measuring 85'x3'x58'x9' and is built in brick masonry. The hall has sixteen openings in each storey. The upper storey which is accessible through a staircase on the north-west corner has a running gallery. The centre of the main hall of the lower storey is occupied by a platform built in white marble inlaid with black in geometrical patterns.

## 10. GURDWARA AT RAMPUR KALAN, POLICE STATION BARKI

Guru Har Gobind visited this village and in memory of his visit a gurdwara was built in the suburb of the village.

### RAWALPINDI DISTRICT

## 11. GURDWARA AT NIRALI, TAHSIL GUJAR KHAN

Har Bans, a saintly disciple of Guru Har Gobind, lived at this village. Once Guru Har Gobind came here to see him. This gurdwara was built in memory of his visit to the place.

### SHEIKHUPURA DISTRICT

## 12. GURDWARA AT NANKANA; (Pl. No. 47)

Once Guru Har Gobind went to Nankana to pay a visit to the shrines associated with Guru Nanak. Later a gurdwara was built over the place where he resided during his stay.

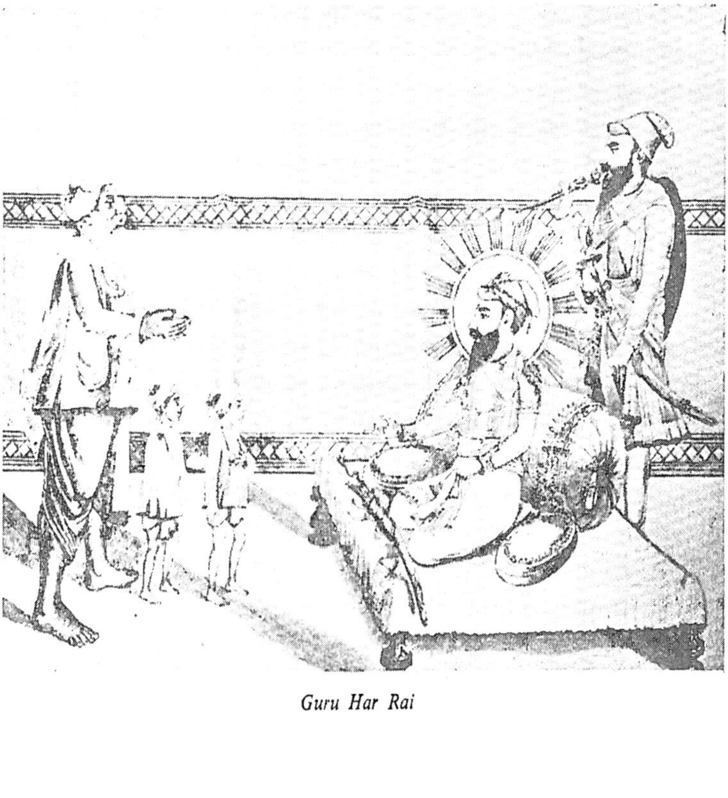

*Guru Har Rai*

PLATE NO. 48.

## GURU HAR RAI—THE 7TH GURU

## (1631—1661)

Born in 1631, Har Rai, son of Gurditta, son of the 6th Guru Har Gobind, succeeded his grand-father when only fourteen years of age. He was a peace loving man and is said to have good relations with Prince Dara Shikoh, the eldest son of Emperor Shahjahan. During the war of succession when Dara Shikoh was fleeing towards the Punjab, Guru Har Rai is said to have checked the troops of Aurangzeb in order to give Dara Shikoh time to flee. After the execution of Dara Shikoh in 1659 A. D. Aurangzeb summoned the Guru to Delhi for an explanation. Guru Har Rai, however, did not go in person to the Mughal Court and instead sent his elder son Ram Rai to explain matters. Ram Rai pleaded his father's case so successfully that Aurangzeb was much pleased and favoured him with due honours. Guru Har Rai died at Kartarpur in 1661 A.D. leaving two sons from his four wives. Before his death he nominated his younger son Har Krishan, a child of six years, as his successor in preference to his elder son Ram Rai.

No sacred monument associated with Guru Har Rai is situated in Pakistan.

## GURU HAR KRISHAN—THE 8TH GURU

## (1656—1664 A.D.)

Har Krishan, younger son of Har Rai, became Guru in 1661 A.D., when he was about six years of age. But Ram Rai, his elder brother, who was at Delhi did not favour this succession. A dispute arose among the rival claimants for the 'Guruship' and the issue became so serious that it was finally referred to the Emperor Aurangzeb who summoned Har Krishan to his Court with the intention that the two brothers should decide the issue peacefully. Aurangzeb was so much struck with Har Krishan's intellect and power of observation that he decided the Guruship in his favour. But the young Guru before leaving Delhi was attacked by small-pox and died in 1664 A.D.*

No sacred place associated with him is situated in Pakistan.

*According to another version he died on 9th April, 1665 A.D.

*Guru Har Krishan*

PLATE NO. 49.

*Guru Tegh Bahadur*

PLATE NO. 50.

## GURU TEGH BAHADUR—THE 9TH GURU

## (1622—1675 A.D.)

Guru Har Krishan at the time of his death, is said to have alluded that his successor would be found in a village called Bakala near Govindwal on the Beas river. Here was born Guru Tegh Bahadur, the youngest son of the sixth Guru, Har Gobind, from his wife Nanaki in Samvat 1679 (A.D. 1622). Tegh Bahadur married Gujari, daughter of Lal Chand of Kartarpur in District Jallundhar and after the death of his father settled down at Bakala with his wife and mother. When approached, Tegh Bahadur first refused the Guruship as the Sodhis (the clan to which all the provious gurus belonged) had already proclaimed a Guru of their own and Ram Rai, elder son of Guru Har Rai was also pressing his claim to the Guruship. At last, Tegh Bahadur was prevailed upon by the repeated requests of his mother and was proclaimed the head of the Sikh Community. On becoming Guru he asserted that he was not worthy of his father's sword and would therefore like to be called as Degh Bahadur (one who excells at tables). He left Bakala and settled at Makhoval on the bank of Sutlej near Kartarpur. Makhoval on becoming the residence of the Guru, came to be known as Anandpur. After sometime, accompanied by his wife, Guru Tegh Bahadur went on pilgrimage to Patna where he stayed for five-six years. It was during his stay at Patna that the tenth Guru was born. At Patna, Guru Tegh Bahadur, received from local pandits his first discourse on Hindu teachings and religious practices which deeply influenced his mind.

Guru Tegh Bahadur's accession had caused many dissensions. Formidable amongst the rival claimant to the Guruship was Ram Rai, son of Guru Har Rai who continued to assert his claim and is said to have poisoned Aurangzeb's mind against Guru Tegh Bahadur. The other rival was his nephew Dhir Mal, son of Gurditta. Aurangzeb, influenced by Ram Rai, summoned Guru Tegh Bahadur to Delhi but the Guru escaped to Assam with the help of Ram Singh son of Jai Singh I, the Raja of Jaipur. According to another account it was Raja Bir Singh who had helped the Guru.

Guru Tegh Bahadur on account of his organizing capacity was able to muster a large well-equipped force and was determined to establish an independent rule. To achieve his goal he formed a league with Shaikh Adam Hafiz a disciple and successor of Faqir Shaikh Farid II. The Guru is said to have levied contributions on rich Hindus while his confederate did the same on wealthy Muslims and thus they started interfering with the sovereign power. The imperial troops therefore marched, defeated and captured both of them.

On his way to Delhi, Guru Tegh Bahadur is said to have sent for his young son Gobind and appointed him his successor. Girding the sword of Guru Har Gobind he hailed him as the Guru of the Sikhs. He gave the new Guru necessary instructions to follow his policy and at Delhi he met his death in 1675 A.D. about which the accounts differ. According to one version he was summoned before the emperor who asked him to perform a miracle in proof of his divine power which he exercised as the head of the Sikhs. The Guru is said to have answered that the performance of miracles incurs God's wrath and that the duty of man was only to pray to his Lord. Thereupon he was confined and told that he would not be released unless he performed a miracle. When tired of the rigours of confinement, the Guru said that he would write a charm and place it around his neck and will then allow a sword to fall on it. The charm will prevent any harm to him. Accordingly he placed the charm around his own neck and bent his head. A blow, however, severed it to the surprise of all those present on the occasion. On the so called charm was found written '*Sar Diya, Sirr na diya*' i.e. gave the head but not the secret.

The earliest reference in support of this version is found in a manuscript copy of Guru Granth written in 1732 Bikrami (1675 A.D.) and quoted by Sardar J.B. Singh, retired Post Master General, in his book '*Parachin Beran*' page 219. It may be added that this is the year in which the Guru met his death. In this work the event has been referred to in a brief manner rather in an alluded form. It records that in Bikrami 1732 in Delhi Guru Tegh Bahadur gave his life in a song i.e. a dramatic action. This is obviously a reference to the story of the charm. This is the earliest reference to the Guru's death. The same version has been stated in details in *Umdatut Tawarikh* by Lala Sohan Lal Suri, a Vakil at the Sikh Court of Lahore written in Samvat 1826 (1871 A.D.)

It is also mentioned that the Guru despaired of his life and tired of prison asked one of his followers to severe his head who first hesitated to do so, but when he was told by the Guru that it was no sin or cruelty on his part, instead that action of his would bring him nearer to the Guru, he, the follower, acted upon the direction and severed the Guru's head.

Acçount of this version has been given by Bhai Muni Singh in his book *Bhagat Ratna Waali*, published in 1893, pages 165-166 but originally written much earlier, perhaps towards the end of 17th century A.D. Bhai Muni Singh when a child of five was given by his father Chaudhri Daulat to Guru Tegh Bahadur and since then remained in service of Guru Gobind Singh who threw light on the death of Guru Tegh Bahadur.

The same version has been given in *Guru Bilas Patshahi Chai Adhyai* by Kavi Sohan Singh. This book was completed in 1775 Bikrami (1718 A.D.) i.e. after 42 years of the death of the Guru. This version is also repeated in *Guru Bilas Patshahi Das* written in Bikrami 1854 (1797 A.D.) by Sukha Singh (1767-1838 A.D.) and followed up by Major Henry Court in his "History of Sikhs", written in 1868 A.D. page 38. The same version has been given in the Adi Granth by Dr. Earnest Trumpp, London 1877 page LXXXVII-III.

Some authorities allege that the Guru was put to death under order of Aurangzeb on charges of treason and disturb ng the peace of the realm.

The earliest reference to this version appears in *Khulasatut Tawarikh* of Munshi Sujan Rai Bhandari of Batala written in 1107 A.H. (1695-96 A.D.) i.e. after 20 years of the event. Sujan Rai says that the Guru was put to death under orders of Aurangzeb in Shahjahanabad in 1081 A.H.

J.D. Cunningham who was in the service of Sikh Government from 1838 A.D. to 1846 A.D. has also expressed the same view.

Max Arthur Macauliffe supporting this view gives more details in his book "The Sikh religion, its Gurus, Sacred Writings and Authors", published from Oxford in 1909 at pages 378-387. He says when the Guru with his five Sikhs namely Mati Das, Gurditta, Uda, Chima and Deyala arrived in Delhi the Emperor sent for him and asked him to accept Islam or work a miracle failing which he would be put to death. The Guru remained firm and was therefore executed by Sayyid Adam Shah in the presence of all the courtiers, Muhammadan priests of Delhi and a great crowd, on Thursday of the light half of the month of Maghar in the Samvat year 1732 (A.D. 1675).

Thus according to the early Sikh writers, Kavi Sohan Singh author of *Guru Bilas Patshahi Chai* (completed in 1720 A.D.) Kavi Sukha Singh author of *Guru Bilas Patshahi Das* (completed in 1797 A D ) Umdatut Tawarikh of Lala Sohan Lal of the Sikh Court (completed in

1871 A.D.) as well as Dr. Trumpp who translated Adi Granth in 1877 A.D., Guru Tegh Bahadur tired of his confinement devised his own death by asking to throw a sword on his neck around which was tied a charm written by him. However, Sujan Rai Bhandari in his book Khulasatut Tawarikh (written in 1695-96 A.D.) without giving the details of the event has written that the Guru was put to death under orders of Aurangzeb. Similarly almost all the foreign authors including Major Henri Court (1868), Dr. Trumpp (1777) Max Arthur Macauliffe (1909) are ot the opinion that it was Aurangzeb who caused the death of the Guru. Since this charge has not been levelled by the early Sikh and Hindu writers, it can be concluded that it has been brought against Aurangzeb only by foreigners in pursuit of the political dogma of 'divide and rule' with a view to create religious bias and hatred between the Muslims and Sikhs. A person like Aurangzeb who for reasons of state could imprison his father, kill his own brothers, Dara Shikoh and Murad, disgrace his elder son, Muazzim, could not of course be expected to spare anybody on that account, but the charges of compulsion in matter of religious belief appears to be an invention of the foreign authors and the truth appears to be that intrigues and enmity of Guru's near relatives like Ram Rai son of Guru Har Rai and his nephew Dhir Mal son of Gurditta and Guru's own desire for rule brought him in conflict with the state which resulted in his death.

*Guru Gobind Singh*

PLATE NO. 51.

## GURU GOBIND SINGH—THE 10TH GURU

## (1665—1708 A.D.)

Guru Gobind Singh, born at Patna in 1665 A.D. was only ten years of age *when he succeeded his father. Guru Gobind Singh spent his early life in retirement in lower hills of the Punjab occupying himself in hunting, studying history, Sanskrit and Persian literature and military science. During these years he is also said to have performed an austere devotion to Durga Devi at Maina Devi hills. But according to his own statement he was busy in the translation of *Ram Avatar*.

The death of his father deeply moved him and he felt the necessity of raising a strong force to take revenge. To achieve this end he made radical changes in Sikh ritual and polity. He renamed the Sikhs as Khalsas—the pure. The Khalsa were to worship Akalpurkh (God) only; pay homage to the Granth alone; be free from caste prejudices and take baptism of water stirred with a dagger. For unity and singleness of purpose among his followers he introduced and made compulsory the use of *Kes* (unshorn hair), *Kachh* (drawers reaching only knee), *Kara* (steel bracelet), *Kirpan* (small dagger) and *Kangha* (comb) known as five *Kakas* in Sikh religious terminology. Renouncing the Hindu title of Rai, he adopted the specific surname of *Singh* (lion); introduced a new form of salutation and prohibited smoking. With a view to strengthen his power and to have safe resorts against Imperial forces, he built three strongholds at Anandpur, Chaundkaur and Paunta. He resided at Anandpur where a large number of Sikh warriors gathered around him. He called himself *Sachcha Badshah* (real king). As a result of these changes the character of Sikhs underwent radical transformation.

The hardship suffered by Guru Arjun Dev, the imprisonment of Guru Har Gobind, and the death of Guru Tegh Bahadur were sufficient causes to arouse the Sikhs against the ruling power. Guru Gobind Singh took advantage of the situation. The long absence of Emperor Aurangzeb from the capital provided him with an opportunity to finalize his plans undisturbed and enforcement of his religious control helped the

* Cunningham says fifteen but does not mention date of birth.

Guru to rise against the Emperor. His first encounter however, was with the Rajas of the adjoining hill states who fearing the rising power of the Guru had made an alliance against him. In a fierce battle the hill Rajas lost the day. Since the first encounter more battles followed but every time the Guru gained victory over the combined forces of the Rajas. The Rajas thus humiliated approached the Emperor. After repeated attempts they succeeded in persuading the Emperor, to despateh a powerful contingent for the submission of the Guru. This force led by Wazir Khan of Sirhind and Zabardast Khan of Lahore, in collaboration with the hill-Rajas forced the Guru to leave Anandpur. The Guru effected his own escape to Chamkaur but his two sons and his mother are said to have been captured during the flight. It is alleged that the boys were put to death and their grand-mother died of the shock. The Guru reached the stronghold of Chamkaur where he was pursued and beseiged. His remaining two sons died while defending the city whereas he again escaped in the darkness of the night, and reached Khidrana afterwards known as Muktesar in Ferozpur District. A strong body of his followers gathered around him and he was able to raise a fresh force determined to face the situation with zeal and courage. Wazir Khan of Sarhind came to know about the new designs of the Guru and sent a detachment against him. In the encounter which followed, the Guru's forces suffered heavy losses and he escaped to Talwandi Sahi (now known as Damdama Sahib) in Patiala. For sometime he remained in seclusion and composed the supplementary Granth.

Aurangzeb died in 1707 A.D. Guru Gobind Singh became friendly with Bahadur Shah who succeeded his father. After sometime he joined the Mughal army and proceeded towards south with the Royal standard until the army reached Nander, about 150 miles north-west of the present city of Hyderabad. Here the Guru settled permanently and started religious activities. He met Lachman Dev later known as Banda. The Guru died at Nander in 1708 A.D. at the hands of a grieved person whose father is said to have been killed by the Guru. Before his death he called for his disciples snd gave his last injunction. Henceforth the Khalsa were enjoined to look upon the Granth Sahib as the living Guru as no new Guru was to come after him.

No sacred place associated with this Guru is situated in Pakistan.

*CHAPTER II*

# OTHER SHRINES

*The following shrines and Samadhs though not directly associated with the Gurus, but sacred to the Sikhs are described below:—*

## ATTOCK DISTRICT

### 1. GURDWARA AT KOT BHAI THAN SINGH; (Pl. No. 52)

Bhai Than Singh was a famous Saint who settled at Kot Fatah Khan. The Muslim Landlord of the village was much impressed by his religiosity and devotion to God and served the saint with respect. The village was named Kot Bhai Than Singh after the saint's name and a gurdwara was built there during the Sikh Rule.

## BANNU DISTRICT

### 2. DHARAMSALA OF UTAM SINGH AT DHARMA KHEL

### 3. JOGIWARA OF SHER NATH AT VILLAGE BAZAR AHMED KHAN

### 4. MAKHAN SHAH SHRINE AT SHEIKH BUDIN HILLS

## DERA ISMAIL KHAN DISTRICT

### 5. DHARAMSALA AT DERA ISMAIL KHAN

It is situated in Chotta Bazar and is a popular religious centre of the town.

### 6. GURDWARA AMAR SHAH SINGH, DERA ISMAIL KHAN

The Gurdwara is situated in Jhanda Ram street and according to the inscription on the foundation stone it was founded in 1895 A.D.

## 7. GURDWARA KALI DEVI, DERA ISMAIL KHAN

It is situated outside Topanwala Gate.

## GUJRANWALA DISTRICT

## 8. SAMADH OF SARDAR CHARRAT SINGH, GUJRANWALA; (Pl. No. 53)

Sardar Charrat Singh, grandfather of Maharaja Ranjit Singh, established a stronghold at Gujranwala. He was killed in 1722 when his matchlock bursted. A Samadh was built over the place where he was cremated.

## 9. SAMADH OF SARDAR MAHAN SINGH, GUJRANWALA; (Pl. No. 54)

Sardar Mahan Singh, father of Maharaja Ranjit Singh, established his supremacy over other petty chiefs of the Punjab. He, in alliance with Sardar Jassa Singh and Sansar Chand, defeated Jai Singh Kanahya in 1785 A.D. In 1792 A.D., while he beseiged Gujrat, he fell ill and died. His samadh which has a high dome was built by Maharaja Ranjit Singh, over the place where his body was cremated.

## 10. DAMDAMA SAHIB, GUJRANWALA; (Pl. No. 55)

Baba Sahib Singh, a descendant of Guru Nanak, was a famous saint. The platform on which he used to sit is known as Damdama Sahib.

There are two other Gurdwaras at Gujranwala namely Jan Gurdwara at G. T. Road and Gurdwara Akalis near Clock Tower.

## GUJRAT DISTRICT

## 11. GURDWARA BHAI BANNU AT MANGAT, TAHSIL PHALIA; (Pl. No. 56)

Bhai Bannu who was a celebrated disciple of Guru Arjun Dev, the 5th Guru, and who copied the first manuscript of Adi Granth came from this village. A gurdwara was built in memory of this disciple at the spot where the copy of the Granth transcribed by him was preserved.

## HAZARA DISTRICT

### 12. DERA BHAI KIRPA RAM AT KOT NAJIBULLA.

It was a residential place of Bhai Kirpa Ram, a Sikh Saint. A festival, known as "*Bhai Ka Karah*" used to be held here on Baisakhi.

### 13. GURDWARA CHITTI GATTI NEAR MANSEHRA

A festival is held here on the occasion of Baisakhi every year.

### 13 (a) GURDWARA AT MANSEHRA (Pl. No. 57)

This Gurdwara has an imposing building.

## JHANG DISTRICT

### 14. GURDWARA BHAI KHAN CHAND AT MAGHIANA

It is situated in Chambeli Market, Maghiana. Extensive repairs were carried out during the year 1953-54. The Gurdwara is very well maintained.

### 15. GURDWARA BHAI HEMASAIN AT MAGHIANA

It is situated in Mohallah Bhabrana. An annual fair at the birth day of Guru Nanak used to be held here. Repairs to the building had been carried out by the Rehabilitation Department, Government of Pakistan.

### 16. DHARAMSALA, HEMA, JEE, AT MAGHIANA

This Dharamsala provided accommodation to the visitors on the occasion of the fair held in gurdwara Bhai Hema Sain. It was repaired by the Rehabilitation Department Government of Pakistan in 1953-54 and it is in good state of preservation.

### 17. GURDWARA AT BHAWANA, TAHSIL CHINIOT

Repairs to the building have been carried out from time to time and it is in good condition.

### 18. GURDWARA AT THATHA FATEH ALI, TAHSIL CHINIOT.

This gurdwara is in a perfect and sound condition.

## 19. GURDWARA AT NANAK SAR, TAHSIL JHANG

Necessary repairs to this gurdwara were carried out by the Rehabilitation Department, Government of Pakistan.

## JHELUM DISTRICT

Following ten gurdwaras are situated at Jhelum:

20. Gurdwara situated in Shumali Mohalla and is in good condition.
21. Gurdwara situated in Machine Mohalla No. 2.
22. Gurdwara situated in Machine Mohalla No. 3 and is in a good state of preservation.
23. Gurdwara built beside the river bank and is in a fair condition.
24. Gurdwara situated in Bagh Mohalla. It is in good condition.
25. Gurdwara situated in Sabzi Mandi. It is well kept and is in good condition.
26. Gurdwara situated in Sabzi Mandi.
27. Gurdwara situated near the river bank.
28. Gurdwara situated beside the river bank.
29. Gurdwara situated in Bagh Mohalla.

Nine Gurdwaras situated in Chakwal bear the following property numbers:—

30. No. B.I.I. S/15.
31. No. BII-19-S/10.
32. No. BII.-19-S/19
33. No. BII-4-S/12
34. No. BIII-8-S/3
35. No. BIII-9-S/43
36. No. BIV-1-S/74
37. No. BVII-2-S/18
38. No. BVII-2-S/77

## KOHAT DISTRICT

## 39. GURDWARA AT KOHAT CANTONMENT

This gurdwara is in a good state of preservation.

## 40. GURDWARA SINGH SABHA

It is in good condition.

# LAHORE DISTRICT

## 41. GURDWARA AND SAMADH AT BHAI PHERO; (Pl. No. 58)

Once Sangatia, later known as Bhai Phero, was passing near Kartarpur, with hides of ghee. A supervisor of Guru Har Rai purchased the ghee and it was agreed that the payment would be made on the following day. The ghee was delivered and empty hides were retained by Sangatia. Next day he found the hides again filled with ghee. He was rather amazed at this miracle and on his enquiry from Bhagtu he was introduced to Guru Har Rai whose spiritual powers had caused the miracle. Guru converted him and gave the title 'phero' and prayed that God may enable him to maintain a langarkhana to supply food to every stranger.

Once Guru Gobind Singh ordered all the *masands* or the collectors of religious taxes to give proper account of their respective collections as a large number of Sikhs had reported against their dishonesty. Bhai Phero who was then the collector of Naka, the country between rivers Ravi and Beas, was also summoned. On finding his account in order he was awarded a robe of honour. He died at a village now known after his name as Bhai Phero.

The present smadah built during the later Sikh period occupies the place where there was originally a small Marhi—A Langar Khana standing nearby is also attached to it. About two thousand acres of agricultural land is attached to the shrine. The management of the estate and smadh is under the local Panchayat Committee.

## 42. GURDWARA AT KAHNA, TAHSIL LAHORE; (Pl. No. 59)

Baba Jamiat Singh, a saint of the nineteenth century, used to sit in meditation at the site of the present gurdwara. The Sikhs of the area had great faith in him. After his death a samadh was constructed on the spot which was later on converted into a samadh-cum-gurdwara. The building, square in plan, has panelled facades with two ornamental false balconies on each side. A door in the middle of each side leads into the interior where a number of rooms are built round a central chamber which is the samadh proper, surmounted with a squat fluted dome the base of which is decorated with naga head design. There is also a well near the 'Dewrhi'. Five hundred acres of agricultural land is attached to the gurdwara and a fair used to be held at this place every month.

## 43. DERA BABA KHUDA SINGH, LAHORE; (Pl. No. 60)

Jaswant Singh, afterwards known as Baba Khuda Singh, was a famous saint of nineteenth century. He was a great traveller and lived for a long time at Kabul where he was well treated by Amir Dost Muhammad Khan. He is held in high esteem by the Sikhs.

Dera Baba Khuda Singh, situated in Chuna Mandi Bazar, adjacent to Diwan Khana, is a Sikh period building, built in cut brick work with panelled facade. The entire area occupied by the Dera measures 57'x67'. The centre of this area is occupied by a courtyard measuring 42'-6"x 31'-3". This courtyard is surrounded by five residential rooms on the north-east side and three shops in north west side. The main sanctuary is a hall occupied by a marble pavilion (5'-6"x3'-3") with a curvilineal roof. The pavilion was most probably the seat of the Granth Sahib. The hall and a room on the west are paved with marble tiles. The main entrance to the samadh is on the Rarra Talian side on the north. Three sky lights were built in the facade facing north.

## 44. SHAHID GANJ (PLACE OF MARTYRS); (Pl. No. 61)

This is situated just east of the Landa Bazar, outside the Delhi Gate, in the neighbourhood of Sultan ki Sarai. This locality including the Landa Bazar and Sultan ki Sarai is the old side of the Chowk of Dara Shikoh, the eldest son of Shahjahan. Situated in this area were the palaces of Dara Shikoh, a garden, a two storeyed Katra or Bazar and a Nakkhas i.e. horse-market. The chowk was entered through beautiful lofty gates decorated with enamelled tiles.

On the western end and adjacent to Nakkhas a three-domed mosque was constructed in A.H. 1064 (1653 A.D.) by Abdullah Khan, Khan-e-Zaman of Dara Shikoh and later on Kotwal (Police chief) of Lahore during the reign of Aurangzeb. Towards the middle of 18th century A.D. these quarters were plundered and pillaged by unscrupulous looters. Later, they became the victim of the Kashmiri brick sellers who demolished the ruined buildings for selling their bricks. Finally in the beginning of British Period, the area was auctioned to one Muhammad Sultan, a contractor, who completely demolished and cleared the remains including the north gate of Nakkhas which was still standing on the patterns of the entrance gate of Wazir Khan's mosque.

Out of the complex of Chowk Dara Shikoh the Nakkhas mentioned above was destined to be an important historical place. It so happened that during the Viceroyalty of Yahya Khan, Diwan Lakhpat

Rai, inflicted a defeat on the Sikhs near Eminabad. He brought back with him many Sikh prisoners to Lahore and to avenge the death of his brother Jaspat Rai who fell fighting against Sikhs, these prisoners were put to death in the Nakkhas. Why this spot was selected for their assassination is not known. Ranjit Singh enclosed this spot and converted into a sacred place. Inside the enclosure some buildings and memorials were set up and it was named as Shahid Ganj (place of martyrs). Among the memorials erected, there were the samadhs of Bhai Taru Singh and Dhanna Singh, the notables who died at the hands of Lakhpat Rai. In the same enclosure were also the samadhs of Bhai Mani Singh, a punjabi poet, and Bhai Gulzar Singh followers of Guru Gobind Singh who died here in A.H. 1140 (1727 A.D.). But these structures have disappeared long since and it is not known who dismantled them. It is mentioned by Latif that the spot where the rest of the Sikhs died was marked with a high dome with a golden pinnacle as well as some rooms, cells and temple.

## 45. SAMADH OF BHAI VASTI RAM, LAHORE; (Pl. No. 62)

Bhai Vasti Ram was the spiritual guide of Maharaja Ranjit Singh. He died at Lahore and his samadh was built adjacent to the northern defence wall of Old Fort. Built in marble the samadh is a small architectural monument of some beauty.

## 46. SAMADH OF JAMADAR KHUSHAL SINGH

Jamadar Khushal Singh, the Prime Minister of Maharaja Ranjit Singh, died in 1844 A.D. His Samadh is situated outside Masti Gate and occupies the place where he was cremated.

## 47. SAMADH OF MAHARAJA RANJIT SINGH, LAHORE; (Pl. No. 63)

Maharaja Ranjit Singh (1780-1839) was the most powerful Sikh ruler of Punjab. He ruled from 1799 to 1839 A.D. His samadh lies just opposite the Fort on its west and occupies the spot where he was cremated. The construction of the samadh was commenced by his son Kharak Singh, but could not be completed till about 1848 A.D. when the infant Sikh Raja Dalip Singh was deposed and taken to England by the British. Built in brick with a sprinkling of red sandstone and marble, it is a mixture of Hindu and Muslim architecture. The square roof with a central fluted dome is crowded alround with Naga hood designs, generally misunderstood as acanthus leaves, kioska, stone lanterns, and cupolas. The ceilings are decorated with glass mosaic work or plain glass work which is beautiful and has been done skilfully in the main dome. The arches of the interior are of marble strengthened with brickwork and joined with iron clamps. In the centre of sepulchral chamber is a small four columned domed marble pavilion beautifully decorated with pietra dura work wrought in semi-precious stones. In its centre rests a marble urn in the form of lotus containing the ashes of Maharaja. Eleven small marble knobs placed alround hold ashes of four queens and seven slave girls; the remains of the queens being distinguished by a carved representations of pigeons. The interor of the samadh chamber is also decorated with frescoes pertaining to Sikh gurus etc. Two small domed buildings adjacent to and west of the main building con ains the ashes of Kharak Singh, and Nau Nihal Singh and their wives.

The large marble door frame of the main entrance to the samadh proper is decorated with superb pietra dura work.

## 48. SAMADH OF MAHARAJA SHER SINGH, LAHORE; (Pl. No. 64)

Maharaja Sher Singh, son of Maharaja Ranjit Singh, who came to power in 1841 A.D., was assassinated by Ajit Singh of Sindhian Wala on 15th September, 1843 A.D. His samadh situated on the west of Maharaja Ranjit Singh's Samadh, is a simple shrine of brick masonry.

West of the samadh of Sher Singh is the samadh of his wife Randhavi. Over the archway of this building the following inscription is inscribed

سمادھ رانی صاحبہ رندھاوی دھرم کور۔ مہاراجہ شیرسنگھ صاحب بہادر کی
سرگباشی بیوی در ماہ ۱۰- سمت ۱۹۲۷ یوم یکشنبہ

East of Sher Singh's samadh is the samadh of his another wife Rani Partab Kaur. The gateway bears the following inscription:

رانی پرتاب کور والدہ سردار ٹھاکر سنگھ زوجہ مہاراجہ شیرسنگھ بہادر
سرگباشی دھم ماہ بارو سمت ۱۹۱۲

## 49. SAMADHS OF RAJA SUCHET SINGH AND UDHAM SINGH; (Pl. No. 65).

Raja Suchet Singh fell fighting against his nephew Raja Hira Singh in the mausoleum of Mian Wadda. Udham Singh, eldest son of Maharaja Gulab Singh, died in an accidental fall of a portion of masonry work while passing the Roshani Gate. Both the samadhs are situated in the same courtyard near the samadh of Maharaja Ranjit Singh.

## 50. SAMADH OF RAJA TEJA SINGH; (Pl. No. 66)

Raja Teja Singh, a Commander in Sikh army, died in 1863 A.D. His samadh, situated outside Masti Gate, was built under the superintendence of Rai Mul Singh.

## 51. SAMADH OF SARDAR JAWAHIR SINGH; (Pl. No. 67)

Sardar Jawahir Singh was the brother of Rani Jindan, wife of Maharaja Ranjit Singh. He was killed by the Sikh army towards the end of 1844 A.D. Rani Jindan was deeply moved by the death of her brother and mourned heavily over his dead body. His samadh situated outside the Masti Gate, was built by her.

## 52. THAKHURDWARA OF RAJA TEJA SINGH, LAHORE; (Pl. No. 68)

Raja Teja Singh was a general in Sikh army and held the command in a campaign against the British. He died in 1863 A.D. The Thakurdwara situated at the end of Moti Bazar is a double storey building. The courtyard is entered through a door in the north by a flight of steps. The walls inside the temple are decorated with stone carvings. The tower of the temple is a lofty parallelogram of three storeys, the lowest being a double dome. The top of the tower is embellished with a golden pinnacle.

# LYALLPUR DISTRICT

## 53. GURDWARA SHAHID SARDAR DALIP SINGH AT CHAK NO. 132/R, POLICE STATION CHAK JHUMRA.

The gurdwara is visited by the Sikhs every year. It is maintained by the Rehabilitation Department, Goverment of Pakistan.

## 54. GURDWARA SHRI NARAIN DAS JI AT GARH FATAH SHAH

The identity of Shri Narain Das is obscure. The gurdwara after his name is in good condition.

In the centre of the court stands the lofty temple built on a high platform.

# MARDAN DISTRICT

## 55. DERA BABA KARAM SINGH, NEAR MARDAN

Baba Karam Singh who was employed in the British Army as

Dafadar, was a religious minded person. Resigning from the army he settled at this place where he occupied himself in meditation and acquired the reputation of a saint. The Sikhs and Hindus both respected him.

The Dera Sahib, is situated north west of Mardan city at a distance of one and a half miles and occupies the place of his residence.

## MONTGOMERY DISTRICT

There are seven gurdwaras in this district:

**56. GURDWARA AT AJIT SAR.**

**57. GURDWARA AT ARIFWALA.**

**58. GURDWARA AT CHICHA WATNI**

**59. GURDWARA IN GRAIN MARKET, MONTGOMERY.**

**60. GURDWARA SAT SINGH, MONTGOMERY.**

**61. GURDWARA SINGH SABHA, MONTGOMERY.**

**62. SAMADH BABA KARTAR SINGH BEDI.**

## PESHAWAR DISTRICT

### 63. GURDWARA AT JAMRUD; (Pl. No. 69)

Sardar Hari Singh Nalwa was a Sikh general in Maharaja Ranjit Singh's army. During his governorship at Hazara he strengthened the Sikh Rule in this area. On 30th April 1837 A.D., Muhammad Akbar Khan, son of Dost Muhammad Khan, Amir of Kabul, attacked the Sikh post at Jamrud. Hari Singh Nalwa who was commanding the Sikh Army, fought bravely but was fatally wounded. Later a samadh and gurdwara was built in his memory.

### 64. SAMADH OF BHAI PHOLA SINGH AT NOWSHERA; (Pl. No. 70)

Akali Phola Singh was a noble from Amritsar and held a responsible post in Maharaja Ranjit Singh's army. He fell fighting against Pathans at Nowshera on 14th March, 1829. A magnificient building was raised on the spot where his body was cremated.

### 65. GURDWARA JOGAN SHAH AT PESHAWAR; (Pl. No. 71)

Jogan Shah was a saintly person respected equally by the Muslims, Hindus and Sikhs. On his death a gurdwara was raised by the Sikhs as a token of reverence.

## RAWALPINDI DISTRICT

### 66. DARBAR BABA KHEM SINGH; (Pl. No. 72)

This darbar was built by the late Sir Baba Khem Singh, the spiritual head of the Potwar Sikhs and a member of Legislative Council. He lived in Kallar in Kahuta Tahsil. The building is in good condition.

### 67. GURDWARA BHAI MANNI SINGH

This gurdwara is situated in Bazar Sarrafan and is held sacred by the Sikhs.

### 68. GURDWARA NARANKARI, RAWALPINDI; (Pl. No. 73)

This gurdwara situated in the market near Raja Bazar is said to have been built by Ram Kanwar, a descendant of Bhai Budha, better known as Bhai Gurbakhsh Singh. He was favoured by Guru Gobind Singh who gave him phul or baptism by the dagger and awarded him the title of Bhai Gurbaksh Singh. He died in 1733 A.D. The gurdwara is held in high esteem by Narankari Sikhs.

### 69. GURDWARA SINGH SABHA RAWALPINDI; (Pl. No. 74)

This gurdwara situated in Raja Bazar, has a massive and imposing building. It is held in high esteem by Akali Sikhs.

### 70. GURDWARA SIRI DAYAL SAR AT TOPY RAKH; (Pl. No. 75)

The gurdwara is situated at a picturesque spot. It was also built by Bhai Gurbakhsh Singh Narankari. It is also held in high esteem by Narankari Sikhs. Large scale repairs to this building by the Pakistan Government have improved its general view.

## SARGODHA DISTRICT

There are three gurdwaras in this district:

### 71. GURDWARA IN BLOCK NO. 3, SARGODHA

### 72. GURDWARA IN BLOCK NO. 2, SARGODHA

### 73. GURDWARA AT BHERA.

## SIALKOT DISTRICT

### 74. GURDWARA AT GLOTIAN KHURD, TAHSIL DASKA; (Pl. No. 76)

It is one of the famous gurdwaras of the district and the Sikhs visited it from far and wide. A fair used to be held here annually.

### 75. GURDWARA TALI (SHISHAM) SAHIB AT SALEHPUR, TAHSIL SIALKOT.

A Sikh visited this place and it was due to his prayers that a dried shisham tree, becamo green. The Sikhs constructed a gurdwara which is known as Tali Sahib after the tree.

## SUKKUR DISTRICT

There are two gurdwaras in this district both situated at Rohri.

### 76. GURDWARA BHAI TERIA SINGH KANDHERA.

### 77. GURDWARA JENRIAN SINGH KANDHERA.

## THARPARKAR DISTRICT

There are six Sikh Shrines and gurdwaras:

### 78. GURDWARA AT SHAHI BAZAR

### 79. GURDWARA AT DIGRI

### 80. GURDWARA AT JHUDO

### 81. GURDWARA AT JHUDO

### 82. GURDWARA AT JHUDO

### 83. GURDWARA AT TANDO JAN MUHAMMAD.

## GENEALOGICAL TABLE OF SIKH GURUS

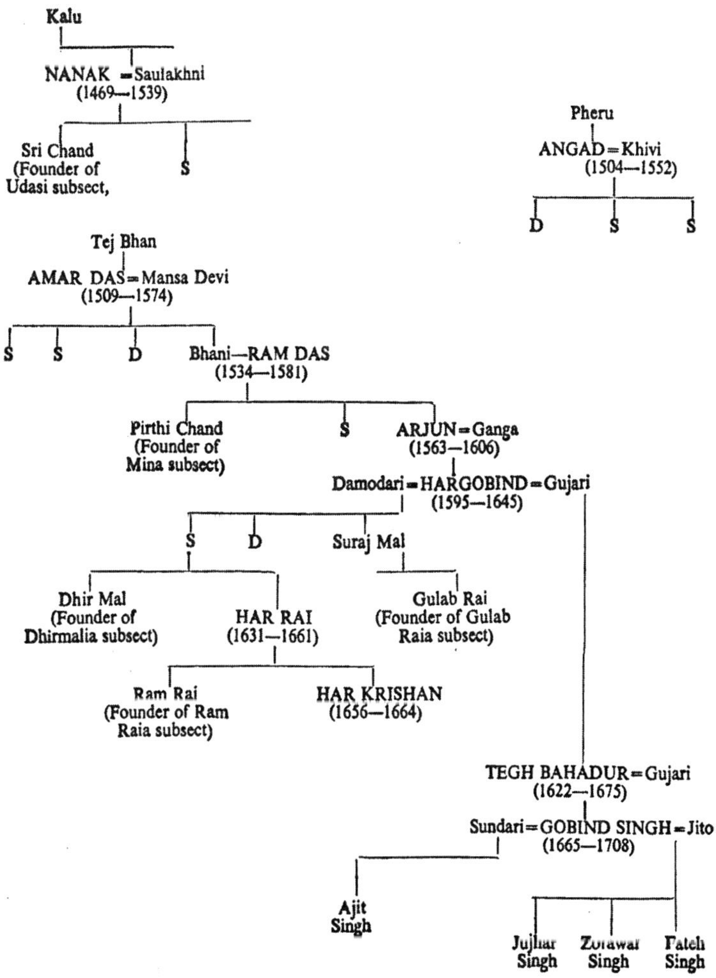

## LIST OF SIKH SHRINES IN WEST PAKISTAN.

| S. No. | District | Locality | Name of Shrine |
|---|---|---|---|
| 1. | Attock | Kot Bhai Than Singh | Gurdwara Bhai Than Singh |
| 2. | Do | Hasan Abdal | Panja Sahib |
| 3. | Bannu | Dharma Khel | Dharam Sala Utam Singh |
| 4. | Do | Vi: Bazar Ahmed Khan | Jogiwara of Sher Nath |
| 5. | Do | Sheikh Budin Hills | Makhan Shah Shrine |
| 6. | D. I. Khan | D. I. Khan | Dharam Sala Nankiana |
| 7. | Do | Do | Gurdwara Amar Shah Singh |
| 8. | Do | Do | Gurdwara Kali Devi |
| 9. | Gujranwala | Eminabad | Chaki Sahib |
| 10. | Do | Gujranwala | Damdama Sahib |
| 11. | Do | Hafizabad | Gurdwara |
| 12. | Do | Wazirabad | Guru Ka Koth |
| 13. | Do | Eminabad | Khoi Bhai Lalu |
| 14. | Do | Do | Rori Sahib |
| 15. | Do | Gujranwala | Samadh of Sardar Charrat Singh |
| 16. | Do | Do | Samadh of Sardar Mahan Singh |
| 17. | Gujrat | Gujrat | Gurdwara |
| 18. | Do | Mangat | Gurdwara Bhai Bano |
| 19. | Do | Jai Sukh | Kir Sahib |

| S. No. | District | Locality | Name of Shrine |
|---|---|---|---|
| 20. | Hazara | Kot Najib-Ulla | Dera Bhai Kirpa Ram |
| 21. | Do | Near Mansehra | Gurdwara Chitti Chatti |
| 22. | Jhelum | Rohtas | Choa Sahib |
| 23. | Do | Bagh Mohalla Jhelum | Gurdwaras |
| 24. | Do | Do | Do |
| 25-33. | Do | Chakwal | Gurdwaras |
| 34. | Jhelum | Machine Mohalla No. 2 Jhelum | Gurdwara |
| 35. | Do | Machine Mohalla No. 3 Jhelum | Do |
| 36-38. | Do | River Bank Jhelum | Gurdwaras |
| 39-40. | Do | Sabzi Mandi Jhelum | Do |
| 41. | Do | Shumali Moh. Jhelum | Gurdwaras |
| 42. | Jhang | Maghiana | Dharam Sala Hema Jee |
| 43. | Do | Bhawana Tah. Chiniot | Gurdwara |
| 44. | Do | Nanaksar | Do |
| 45. | Do | Thatha Fateh Ali Tah. Chiniot | Do |
| 46. | Do | Maghiana | Gurdwara Bhai Hem Singh |
| 47. | Do | Do | Gurdwara Bhai Khan Chand |
| 48. | Kohat | Kohat Cantt. | Gurdwara |
| 49. | Do | Kohat | Gurdwara Singh Sabha |
| 50. | Lahore | Lahore | Baoli Sahib |
| 51. | Do | Do | Buddhu Ka Awa |
| 52. | Do | Chahal | Dera |

| S. No. | District | Locality | Name of Shrine |
|---|---|---|---|
| 53. | Lahore | Lahore | Dera Baba Khuda Sing |
| 54. | Do | Alpa | Dharam Sala Chhota Nankiana |
| 55. | Do | Manga | Do |
| 56. | Do | Lahore | Dharamsala Sat Guru Nanak |
| 57. | Do | Do | Diwan Khana |
| 58. | Do | Amar Sidhu | Gurdwara |
| 59. | Do | Badhana | Do |
| 60. | Do | Bhai Phero | Do |
| 61. | Do | Dhisalwan | Do |
| 62. | Do | Ghawindi | Do |
| 63. | Do | Guru Mangat | Gurdwara |
| 64. | Do | Hadyarah | Do |
| 65. | Do | Hanjra | Do |
| 66. | Do | Jahman | Do |
| 67. | Do | Jambar Kalan | Do |
| 68. | Do | Kahna | Do |
| 69. | Do | Kanganpura Tah. Chuniyan | Do |
| 70. | Do | Mozang | Do |
| 71. | Do | Rampur Kalan | Do |
| 72. | Do | Lahore | Janam Asthan Guru Ram Das |
| 73. | Do | Do | Lal Khoi |
| 74. | Do | Do | Samadh of Bhai Vasti Ram |
| 75. | Do | Do | Samadh of Guru Arjun Dev. |

| S. No. | District | Locality | Name of Shrine |
|---|---|---|---|
| 76. | Lahore | Lahore | Samadh of Jamadar Khushal Singh |
| 77. | Do | Do | Samadh of Teja Suchet Singh |
| 78. | Do | Do | Samadh of Raja Teja Singh |
| 79. | Do | Do | Samadh of Maharaja Ranjit Singh |
| 80. | Do | Do | Samadh of Maharaja Sher Singh |
| 81. | Do | Do | Samadh of Sardar Jawahir Singh |
| 82. | Do | Do | Shahid Ganj |
| 83. | Do | Do | Thakurdwara Raja Teja Singh |
| 84. | Lyallpur | Chak 132/R.P.S. Chak Jhumra | Gurdwara Shahid Sardar Dilip Singh |
| 85. | Do | Garh Fatah Shah | Gurdwara Shri Narain Das Ji |
| 86. | Mardan | Near Mardan City | Dera Baba Karam Sing |
| 87. | Montgomery | Ajitsar | Gurdwara |
| 88. | Do | Arifwala | Do |
| 89. | Do | Chichawatni | Do |
| 90. | Do | Dipalpur | Do |
| 91. | Do | Grain Market | Do |
| 92. | Do | Tah. Okara | Gurdwara Nanak Jagir |
| 93. | Do | Harappa | Gurdwara Nanaksar |
| 94. | Do | Do | Gurdwara Sat Singh |
| 95. | Do | Montgomery | Gurdwara Singh Sabha |
| 96. | Do | Chak 1/EB Tah. Pakpattan | Gurdwara Tibba Baba Nanak |

| S. No. | District | Locality | Name of Shrine |
|---|---|---|---|
| 97. | Montgomery | Montgomery | Samadh of Kartar Singh Bedi |
| 98. | Multan | Chak 317 Tah. Vehari | Gurdwara Diwan Chawali Mashaykh |
| 99. | Peshawar | Jamrud | Gurdwara |
| 100. | Do | Peshawar | Gurdwara Jogan Shah |
| 101. | Do | Nowshera | Samadh of Bhai Phola Singh |
| 102. | Rawalpindi | .. | Darbar Khem Singh |
| 103. | Do | Nirali | Gurdwara |
| 104. | Do | Rawalpindi | Gurdwara Bhai Manna Singh |
| 105. | Do | Do | Gurdwara Narankari |
| 106. | Do | Do | Gurdwara Singh Sabha |
| 107. | Sialkot | Sialkot | Bairi Sahib |
| 108. | Do | Do | Baoli Sahib |
| 109. | Do | Kartarpur | Darbar Sahib |
| 110. | Do | Glotian Khurd Tah. Daska | Gurdwara |
| 111. | Do | Salehpur Tah. Sialkot | Tali Sahib |
| 112. | Sheikhupura | Nankana | Bal Lila |
| 113. | Do | Haft Madar | Gurdwara |
| 114. | Do | Nankana | Do |
| 115. | Do | Do | Gurdwara Ghhewin Padshahi |
| 116. | Sheikhupura | Nankana | Janam Asthan Guru Nanak |
| 117. | Do | Do | Kiara Sahib |
| 118. | Do | Do | Malji Sahib |

| S. No. | District | Locality | Name of Shrine |
|---|---|---|---|
| 119. | Sheikhupura | Nankana | Moulvi Patti Sahib |
| 120. | Do | Chauharkana | Sachcha Sauda |
| 121. | Do | Nankana | Tambo Sahib |
| 122. | Sargodha | Bhera | Gurdwara |
| 123. | Do | Block No. 2 Sargodha | Do |
| 124. | Do | Block No. 3 Sargodha | Do |
| 125. | Sukkur | Khan Dhera Rohri | Gurdwara Bhai Teria Singh |
| 126. | Do | Rohri | Gurdwara Jenrian Singh |
| 127. | Tharparkar | Digri | Gurdwara |
| 128. | Do | Jhudo | Do |
| 129. | Do | Shahi Bazar | Do |
| 130. | Do | Tando Jan Mohd. | Do |

## SELECT BIBLIOGRAPHY


1. Adi Granth — Translated in English by Dr. Earnest Trumpp, Lodon: W.M.H. Allen, 1877.
2. Fani, Mohsin — Dabistan, translated by D. & A. Troyer, London, 1843.
3. Badayoni, Abdul Qadir — Muntakhabut Tawarikh, edited by Molvi Ahmad Ali, Calcutta, 1869.
4. Khafi Khan — Muntakhabul Lubab, edited by Molvi Kabiruddin Ahmad and Molvi Ghulam Qadir, Calcutta, 1869.
5. Amar Nath, Diwan — Zafar Namah Ranjit Singh, edited by Sita Ram Kohli, Lahore, 1928.
6. Baqir, Dr. Muhammad — Lahore: Past & Present, Lahore, 1952.
7. Khazan Singh — History and Philosophy of the Sikh Religion, Lahore, 1914.
8. Latif, S. Muhammad — Lahore, its History, Architectural Remains and Antiquities, Lahore, n.d.
9. Macauliffe, M.A. — The Sikh Religion, its Gurus, Sacred Writings and Authors. 6 Vols. Oxford, 1909.
10. Malcolm, J. — A Sketch of the Sikhs. London, 1912.
11. Narang, Gokal Chand — Transformation of Sikhism, Lahore.

12. Pin Cott Frederic — Sikhism in its Relation to Muhammadanism, London, 1885.
13. Singh, Khushwant — The Sikhs, London, 1953.
14. Abul Aman Amritsari — Sikh-Muslim Tarikh, Lahore, 1958.
15. Kanhya Lal — Tarikh-e-Lahore, Lahore, 1884.
16. Khushal, Ram Sarup — Das Guru, Lahore, 1929.
17. District Gazetteers of all relevant districts.

# ILLUSTRATIONS

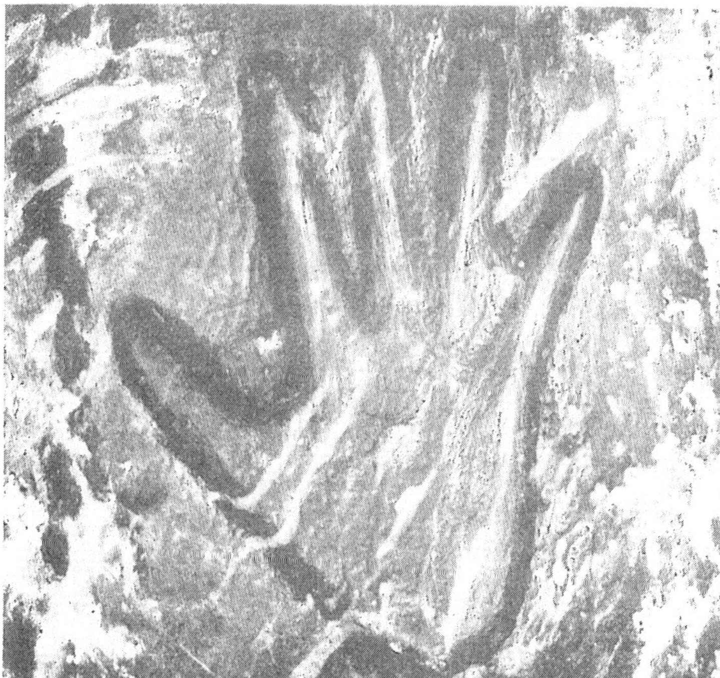

*Hand impression of Guru Nanak at Hasan Abdal*

PLATE NO. 2.

*Modern Building of Panja Sahib at Hasan Abdal*

PLATE NO. 3.

*Chaki Sahib at Eminabad*

PLATE NO. 4.

*Gurdwara Rori Sahib at Eminabad*

PLATE NO. 5.

*Gurdwara Kir at Jai Sukh. Tah. Phalia*

PLATE NO. 6.

*Dharamsala Chhota Nankiana at Alpa*

PLATE NO. 7.

*Dharamsala Chhota Nankiana, Manga*

PLATE NO. 8.

*Entrance of Dharamsala Sat Guru Nanak, Lahore*

PLATE NO. 9.

*Gurdwara and Tank at Village Jahman*

PLATE NO. 10.

*Gurdwara at Ghawindi, P.S. Barki*

PLATE NO. 11.

*Gurdwara at Dipalpur*

PLATE NO. 12.

*Gurdwara Nanak Jagir*

PLATE NO. 13.

*Gurdwara Nanksar at Harappa*

PLATE NO. 14.

*Gurdwara Tibba Baba Nanak Sahib, Chak 1/EB, Tah. Okara*

PLATE NO. 15.

*Gurdwara Diwan Chawali Mashaykh at Chak No. 317, Tah. Vehari*

PLATE NO. 16.

*Gurdwara Bal Lila at Nankana Sahib*

PLATE NO. 17.

*Gurdwara Janam Asthan at Nankana Sahib*

PLATE NO. 18.

*Gurdwara Kiara Sahib at Nankana Sahib*

**PLATE NO. 19.**

*Gurdwara Malji Sahib at Nankana Sahib*

PLATE NO. 20.

*Gurdwara Maulvi Patti at Nankana Sahib*

PLATE NO. 21.

*Gurdwara Sachcha Sauda at Chauharkana*

PLATE NO. 22.

*Gurdwara Tambo Sahib at Nankana Sahib*

PLATE NO. 23.

*Gurdwara Bairi Sahib at Sialkot*

PLATE NO. 24.

*Darbar Sahib at Kartarpur*

PLATE NO. 25.

*Janam Asthan Guru Ram Das at Lahore*

PLATE NO. 29.

*Buddhu Ka Awa at Lahore*

PLATE NO. 31.

*Memorial Gateway of Baoli Sahib at Lahore*

PLATE NO. 32.

*Lal Khoi at Lahore*

PLATE NO. 33.

*Samadh Guru Arjun Dev at Lahore*

PLATE NO. 34.

*Gurdwara at Hanjra*

PLATE NO. 35.

*Gurdwara at Jambar Kalan*

PLATE NO. 36.

*Gurdwara at Haft Madar*



PLATE NO. 37.

*Gurdwara at Hafizabad*

PLATE NO. 39.

*Guru Ka Koth at Wazirabad*

PLATE NO. 40.

*Gurdwara at Gujrat*

PLATE NO. 41.

*Gurdwara at Amar Sidho*

PLATE NO. 42.

*Gurdwara at Badhanà, P.S. Darki*

PLATE NO. 43.

*Gurdwara at Guru Mangat*

PLATE NO. 44.

*Gurdwara at Hadyarah*

PLATE NO. 45.

*Gurdwara at Lahore*

PLATE NO. 46.

*Gurdwara at Nankana Sahib*

PLATE NO. 47.

*Gurdwara at Kot Bhai Than Singh*

PLATE NO. 52.

*Samadh Sardar Charrat Singh at Gujranwala*

PLATE NO. 53.

*Samadh Sardar Mahan Singh at Gujranwala*

PLATE NO. 54.

*Damdama Sahib at Gujranwala*

PLATE NO. 55.

*Gurdwara Bhai Bannu at Mangat, Tah. Phalia*

PLATE NO. 56.

*Gurdwara at Mansehra*

PLATE NO. 57.

*Gurdwara Bhai Phero, Tah. Lahore*

PLATE NO. 58.

*Gurdwara at Kahna, Tah. Lahore*

PLATE NO. 59.

*Darbar Baba Khuda Singh at Lahore*

PLATE NO. 60.

*Shahid Ganj at Lahore*

PLATE NO. 61.

*Samadh of Bhai Vasti Ram at Lahore*

PLATE NO. 62.

*Samadh of Maharaja Ranjit Singh at Lahore*

PLATE NO. 63.

*Samadh of Maharaja Sher Singh at Lahore*

PLATE NO. 64.

*Samadh of Suchet Singh at Lahore*

PLATE NO. 65.

*Samadh of Raja Teja Singh at Lahore*

PLATE NO. 66.

*Samadh of Sardar Jawahir Singh at Lahore*

PLATE NO. 67.

*Thakurdwara of Raja Teja Singh at Lahore*

PLATE NO. 68.

*Gurdwara at Jamrud*

PLATE NO. 69.

*Samadh Bhai Phola Singh at Nowshera*

PLATE NO. 70.

*Gurdwara Jogan Shah at Peshawar*

PLATE NO. 71.

*Darbar Baba Khem Singh*



PLATE NO. 72.

*Gurdwara Narankari at Rawalipndi*

PLATE NO. 73.

*Gurdwara Singh Sabha at Rawalpindi*

PLATE NO. 74.

*Gurdwara Siri Dayalsar at Topy Rakh*

PLATE NO. 75.

*Gurdwara Glotian Khurd*



PLATE NO. 76.

# INDEX

C



D



E



F

G



H



I



J

S



T